W9-BBU-721

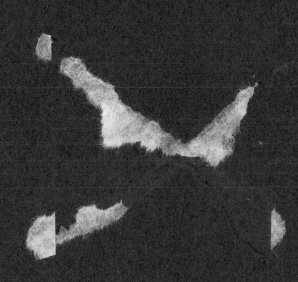

Web of Being

The Novels of Robert Penn Warren

WEB
OF BEING

The Novels of
Robert Penn Warren

BARNETT GUTTENBERG

Vanderbilt University Press
Nashville • 1975

The author and Vanderbilt University Press gratefully acknowledge permission from the publishers to quote from the copyrighted works of Robert Penn Warren, as follows:
RANDOM HOUSE, INC.: *Night Rider, At Heaven's Gate, World Enough and Time, Band of Angels, The Cave, Flood, Wilderness, Meet Me in the Green Glen,* and *Selected Poems: New and Old, 1923–1966.*
HARCOURT BRACE JOVANOVICH, INC.: *All the King's Men.*

8 /3.5 2

498w

96 68 1

april 1976

Library of Congress Cataloguing-in-Publication Data

Guttenberg, Barnett, 1937–
  Web of being: the novels of Robert Penn Warren.
  Bibliography.
  Includes index.
  1. Warren, Robert Penn, 1905–   —Philosophy.
I. Title.
PS3545.A748Z68   813'.5'2   74–26892
  ISBN 0–8265–1198–3

For Ida, John, and Peggy

Contents

Introduction

In his essay on Conrad, Robert Penn Warren defines the "philosophical novelist" as "one for whom the documentation of the world is constantly striving to rise to the level of generalization about values, for whom the image strives to rise to symbol, for whom images always fall into a dialectical configuration, for whom the urgency of experience, no matter how vividly and strongly experience may enchant, is the urgency to know the meaning of experience."[1] It is a truism of sorts that the novelist or poet who ventures into the realm of criticism has as his ultimate subject himself and that he says as much of his own work as of the work he discusses. The purpose of this book is to consider the way in which Warren is in fact speaking of himself when he describes Conrad as "philosophical novelist": to examine the "dialectical configuration" which shapes Warren's vision.

That vision begins with an indictment of the modern world. Like other contemporary analysts of the age, in the fields of philosophy and psychology as well as literature, Warren views the world's chaos as the result of alienation: not the Marxian alienation of the worker, nor even the alienation of the self from society, but the alienation of the self from itself, the dissociation of sensibility traceable to Descartes and even to Plato, in which

---

1. Robert Penn Warren, " 'The Great Mirage': Conrad and *Nostromo*," in *Selected Essays*, p. 58.

man's world is divided against itself into conflicting realms of world and idea, mind and nature. This schism has been of major interest for centuries, but the nineteenth-century Romantics seem to have been the first fully to appreciate its inherent danger. If alienation has become a contemporary cliché, it has perhaps done so because the issue has surfaced with increased urgency.[2]

Warren's critical essays reveal his preoccupation with the divisiveness stemming from that self-alienation. In his essay on Frost, for example, he states, "This theme is one which appears over and over in Frost's poems—the relation . . . between the fact and the dream."[3] In the earlier of his essays on Melville, he speaks of "Melville's concern with the fundamental ironical dualities of existence."[4] Of Hemingway's protagonists, he says, "The violent man is the man taking an action appropriate to the realization of the fact of nada. He is, in other words, engaged in the effort to discover human values in a naturalistic world."[5] Of Wolfe: "He pants for the Word, the union that will clarify all the disparate and confused elements which he enumerates."[6] And, of Conrad's vision: "Wisdom, then, is the recognition of man's condition . . . the necessity of living with the ever renewing dilemma of idea as opposed to nature, morality to action, 'utopianism' to 'secular logic,' . . . justice to material interests."[7] That dilemma is central to Warren's novels as well as to his essays; it is what Jack Burden calls "the terrible division of our age." In the twentieth century, it is the existential writers who have been most concerned with that division, and their formulations are of help in understanding Warren's concerns. Heidegger's philosophy seems particularly applicable, and the following chapters make considerable use of his terminology.

2. For an analysis of this historical development, see William Barrett, *Irrational Man: A Study in Existential Philosophy*, pp. 69–149.
3. Warren, "The Themes of Robert Frost," in *Selected Essays*, p. 124.
4. Warren, "Melville the Poet," in *Selected Essays*, p. 190.
5. Warren, "Ernest Hemingway," in *Selected Essays*, p. 92.
6. Warren, "A Note on the Hamlet of Thomas Wolfe," in *Selected Essays*, p. 180.
7. Warren, " 'The Great Mirage,' " in *Selected Essays*, p. 54.

In Heidegger's view, man is dropped here, left to himself to be as he can in a world of things, a world without meaning. He differs radically from the world in which he finds himself, elevated and isolated by his insistence on meaning. Although he seems superior to the world, in his finitude and limitation he is wholly dependent upon it. This apparent disparity between fact and aspiration, world and idea, constitutes his absurdity. Yet man is not the mere victim of circumstance. He can gain true being—authentic being—by owning up to his limitations and the particular possibilities which they entail; Heidegger's term "authentic being" can also be translated as "owned being" or "acknowledged being." Although one cannot entirely remake his being, he can assume responsibility for it.

The inescapable tendency, however, is for one to fall captive to the world. One does so by giving himself away to things, by disowning his true self and imitating others who seem self-confident and sure: by adopting their possibilities. Alternately, through a process of reaction which Maritain terms "angelism,"[8] he flees from the world into the abstract realm of an ideal, which has invariably been defined by the world he seeks to escape. His flight ends in captivity whether he flees to or from the world, for in either case, he gives his being into the hands of others, while turning away from his own possibilities. Heidegger envisions the process of turning away as a falling away, a surrender to the falling motion of the world. One falls away from true being into a captivating nothingness which is the meaninglessness of the world—both natural and social—without values, and which is always with us, ready to absorb us.

Before a man's being can be authentically his own, he must wrest it back from its lostness to the world, from its fallenness, frequently in its guise of death; he embraces his limitations and thus, his own possibilities; he accepts the responsibility of his freedom. In assuming this responsibility for his being, he cares about and cares for his being, while at the same time he cares about and for the being of others, who share in his struggle. Selfhood, then, stems from an awareness of personal limitation and

8. Jacques Maritain, *The Dream of Descartes,* trans. Mabelle L. Andison.

a resultant sense of the human communion; it involves a new vision of the world, which becomes, not something absurd and separate from man, but man himself in the whole of his possibilities, possibilities which are largely relational.[9]

In Warren's cosmology, as in Heidegger's, man, confronting alternatives of world and idea, must choose neither. He must discover, through the awareness of limitation and the involvement of care, that these alternatives are false: that true being resolves these fragments into a new integrity. Is Warren an existentialist? The vagueness of the term makes the question fruitless. Hazel Barnes, striving to preserve the purity of the term, is forced to fall back upon such designations as "legitimate existentialists" to distinguish the true existentialists, like Sartre, who insists on the inevitable absurdity of man's condition, from the lapsed believers like Heidegger, who, in *Being and Time,* contends that absurdity is surmountable.[10] Is Warren a disciple of Heidegger? Presumably not. Warren's metaphysic may in part reflect the work of any number of existential writers, or it may even be independently derived from a common source: that is, the Christian pattern of conversion. Heidegger's existentialism, after all, is an elaborate but unmistakable version of Christianity secularized, and Warren has called himself "an agnostic Presbyterian."[11]

More important here than such pigeon-holing is the fact that Heidegger's philosophy helps us to define the quest for selfhood as it appears in all of Warren's fiction. Each novel takes its shape from the attempts of its major characters to cope with their own fragmentation. In *Night Rider* and *At Heaven's Gate,* Warren grapples with the problem of alienation and moves toward the solution which he articulates fully in *All the King's*

---

9. The preceding paragraphs present some of the salient points in Martin Heidegger's *Being and Time,* trans. John Macquarrie and Edward Robinson. I have found very helpful Magda King's *Heidegger's Philosophy.*

10. Hazel E. Barnes, *The Literature of Possibility.* For further evidence that, from certain viewpoints, Heidegger is not an existentialist, see John Macquarrie, *Martin Heidegger,* p. 8.

11. Robert Penn Warren in conversation, as reported to the author by Walter Sullivan.

Men; in the subsequent novels, he tests his vision with a variety of characters and situations.

Through all of the novels, the individual attains the true being of selfhood through self-awareness and the realization that, as Warren says in his essay "Knowledge and the Image of Man," he is "in the world with continual and intimate interpenetration, and inevitable osmosis of being, which in the end does not deny, but affirms, his identity. It affirms it, for out of a progressive understanding of this interpenetration, this texture of relations, man creates new perspectives, discovers new values—that is, a new self."[12] The path to this new self begins, with *Night Rider,* in the darkness of Mr. Munn's broken world and ends, with *Meet Me in the Green Glen,* in the great awakening light of Cy Grinder's awareness as Cy discovers the unbroken web which is the world redeemed through knowledge.

12. Robert Penn Warren, "Knowledge and the Image of Man," in *Robert Penn Warren: A Collection of Critical Essays,* ed. John L. Longley Jr., p. 241.

Web of Being

The Novels of Robert Penn Warren

CHAPTER I

Night Rider

PERCY MUNN, the central figure of *Night Rider,* is a type of protagonist grown increasingly familiar to us since 1939, the year in which the novel first appeared. Separated from his comfortable moorings in what had seemed to be a stable society, he finds himself, like Sartre's Roquentin, like Hemingway's Jake or Krebs, cast adrift in emptiness. He discovers that the world, which had seemed fixed, is a thing of flux and chaos: "a violent, swollen stream." He can find no adequate point of reference anywhere and lacks any direction or will. Reluctantly, bullied and cajoled, he comes to the Association meeting, dines with the directors, delivers an extemporaneous speech, and becomes a director. The narrator refers to him throughout as "Mr. Munn;" he is, in one critic's words, "a function or a formal annex, not a man."[1] And in fact he is not Man, but Munn. His problem is simply that he does not wholly exist.

His story arises from his deepening awareness of his own emptiness. When he asks himself, "What was the center of his life?" and admits that "He could not say," he moves beyond emptiness to the perception of emptiness. His quest begins with that awareness, for with it, he is driven to seek some center, some point of reference which will afford him the certainty and definition he

1. Leonard Casper, *Robert Penn Warren: The Dark and Bloody Ground,* p. 106.

sees—or thinks he sees—in others. This search is the quest for
selfhood which informs all of Warren's novels.

At the beginning of *Night Rider,* although Mr. Munn wants
more than anything else to be free, he is caught up in the
mundane. He has his farm, his law practice, his wife, May, and
the promise of a political career. All is indeed sunshine in the
early scenes, but Mr. Munn's life is a veneer, lacking in depth,
and the sunshine, here and throughout Warren's novels, is the
light of objective reality untouched by human values, the light
of the innocence personified in Mr. Munn's wife, May. Mr.
Munn's growing awareness is measured against her innocence,[2]
for whereas he comes to see that "getting older is breaking
through the surfaces" (104), her concern is wholly with surface.
Surveying her work in the garden, Mr. Munn notes that "not
four square feet of the soil was turned up, and that had merely
been pecked at with the useless instrument. As he looked, a sad-
ness overcame him, more than a sadness, a despair that seemed
to well from some profound truth that he had never before sus-
pected." (130)

This anguished view of truth—of the dark center of being—
separates them. The sight of snow, for example, leads May back
to the brightness of her childhood Christmases, when " 'everything, the whole world, would be different. And if there was
snow on the ground, everything would be different.' " (85) May's
nostalgic recollection of a world transformed by snow, like Mr.
Munn's memory of his stereopticon, suggests the childhood innocence into which she withdraws completely when she leaves
Mr. Munn and seeks asylum in the decaying dream house of her
aunt Miss Lucy Burnham's spinsterhood. Mr. Munn's reflections
about the snow, on the other hand, lead in a quite different
direction. He thinks, "Was he staring into blackness, a blackness
external to him and circumambient, or was he the blackness, his
own head of terrific circumference, embracing, enclosing, defining
the blackness, and the effort of staring into the blackness a
staring inward into himself, into his own head which enclosed the

---

2. Charles Bohner, *Robert Penn Warren,* p. 63.

blackness and everything? And enclosed the snow that gently fell in darkness." (109) Mr. Munn sees in the snow, not the child's world of expectation, but a blackness at the very center of life.

Several questions arise at this point. After such knowledge, what forgiveness? Is any form of selfhood possible amid the general disintegration? If so, what keeps Mr. Munn from it?

The possibility of making something out of nothing seems tantalizingly present in the person of Captain Todd, who has a mysterious "deep inner certainty of self" (43) which enables him to stand fast against the chaos of modern life even as he stood fast against the Union onslaught: "aware, it seemed, of a ripe, secret security that he could count on, out of the swirl and reach of the general excitement, supported by a confidence different from the confidence in events and circumstances that would be subject to change and accident and the casual appetites and weaknesses of people." (44) Although Mr. Munn is misled into attributing similar certainty to Senator Tolliver, he makes no mistake about Captain Todd.

Further indication that "certainty of self" is attainable comes later, in the story of Willie Proudfit, who, relating his tale to Mr. Munn, defines the basis of selfhood. Willie begins his spiritual journey in a world like Percy Munn's, a world of turbulent darkness in which Indian and buffalo are systematically annihilated. From this world Willie withdraws into the mountains to live a life of innocence with the Indians. Finally, however, a vision totally antithetical to Mr. Munn's snow vision leads Willie home to the world. In that vision, as he tells Mr. Munn,

They was a fire in me, and thirsten. . . . I come down the hill, and seen houses setten off down the valley, and roofs, and the green trees standen. I taken a bend in the road, and thar was a little church. . . . Thar was a spring thar, by the church, and I seen hit and run to hit. I put my head down to the water, fer the fire in me, lak a dog gitten ready to lap . . . and hit was cool on me. The coolness was in me, and I taken my fill.

No tellen how long, and I lifted up my head. Thar a girl was sitten over thar nigh the spring. (424)

Willie's vision leads him down from his mountain innocence which is suprahuman and heavenly, but at the same time sub-human and damned ("lak a dog gitten ready to leap," "a fire in me"). It leads him into a valley haven which is both fertile and communal ("houses . . . and roofs, and the green trees standen"): and as such, thirst-quenching, life-giving, sacramental. ("Thar was a spring thar, by the church"; "Thar a girl was . . . over thar nigh the spring"). This vision of a world redeemed suggests that selfhood involves the harmonious integration of all things; the dream's improbably coming true suggests that the vision is itself redeeming.

What prevents Mr. Munn from having such a redeeming vision of selfhood? A major part of the novel deals with the pit-falls which impede the modern pilgrim's progress. One of these is the sunlit innocence of Mr. Munn's life when the narrative begins, an innocence which he later tries to regain. Thus, literally sickened by the murder of Bunk Trevelyan, aware that the order of his life is disintegrating, Mr. Munn comes home and attacks May in a frantic attempt to possess her innocence.[3] He fails, of course; her innocence helps to make the act all the more contemptible. He imagines that he can attain "happiness as a thing in itself, an entity separate from the past activities of his life." (160) But as Warren indicates, the man who has taken his first step toward knowledge apparently cannot return to the childhood Eden outside of time.

Another temptation is the worldliness of Senator Tolliver, the flattery and promise of greatness. Tolliver speaks of allegiance to an ideal, an allegiance which "Monclair," the name he has given his home, seems to proclaim. But the palatial aspects of that home, its manifold comforts, reveal that his guiding light is in fact Success. It proves seductive to Mr. Munn throughout, but particularly when he enjoys the comforts of Monclair and when Tolliver lays a paternal hand on his shoulder and promises him greatness. (112)

---

3. But see Casper, *Robert Penn Warren*, p. 106, who argues that Mr. Munn "practices cruelties on his wife in order to feel the assurance of power that absent love is unable to give."

Still another temptation is sexuality. Mr. Munn wants a relationship with Lucille Christian in order to have something stable; "in trying to extract her promise, he was like a man who tries to find in the flux and confusion of data some points of reference, no matter how arbitrary, some hypothesis, on which he can base his calculations." (251) When their romance ends with a meaningless coupling, a variation on the ending of his marriage, "he knew a loathing, suddenly, of himself for the emptiness of the act he had performed. . . . He was infected by her emptiness. Or her emptiness had discovered to him his own." (325) He reaches a partial realization: " 'Love, it's not anything . . . not when it's not a part of something else.' " (440)

Still another temptation is the peace of withdrawal into vegetable insentience represented by Ianthe Sprague. The poem entitled "Ianthe," which Mr. Munn read as a boy in one of his father's books, characterizes her perfectly. He recalls one stanza:

> From you, Ianthe, little troubles pass
> Like little ripples down a sunny river;
> Your pleasures spring like daisies in the grass,
> Cut down, and up again as blithe as ever. (209)

Mr. Munn comes to see that the poem's saccharine romanticism is ludicrously inappropriate to the dirty little old lady, but he fails to realize that its escapism—evident in its minimization of the reaper—is completely characteristic of her. When, as a law student, he tries to read to her, he discovers the scope of her repudiation: "What she liked was the short, flat statement that had no possible reference to her life, advertisements of merchandise which she could neither buy nor use . . . the fragmentary, the irrelevant, the meaningless." (212) Only after considerable contact does he grow to appreciate "the magnitude of her achievement" in isolating herself so completely from the world.

A part of the novel deals with Mr. Munn in a similar state of insentience. After May leaves him, he "thought rather often about Miss Sprague." (214) At one point, he is intrigued with the flight of the grackles south, a flight which the narrator of one of Warren's poems interprets as an attempt to escape the harshness of reality.[4] Later, forced into flight himself, he "sank when possible into a blank absorption with the fact of the moment." (218–219)

But Mr. Munn's major temptation proves to be neither innocence, nor worldliness, nor sexuality, nor withdrawal and submission; the temptation that instigates his quest is the ideal of Justice. The novel gets under way when Mr. Munn, apparently just out of law school, is taken with the ideal of Justice in the form of fair prices for tobacco growers and acquittal for Trevelyan. The ideal seems to provide a clean, well-lighted place amid the surrounding darkness; Mr. Munn, about to address a group of prospective Association members, thinks, "It was almost a mystery, a mystery whose profoundness drew him as he stood there, that he and those men should be together in that little cubicle of comforting warmth and light while the rain and darkness and wind prevailed over the land outside." (39) The ideal is momentarily exciting; Mr. Munn reflects, "An idea—that was it—an idea seized parts of their individual beings and held them together and made them coalesce." (16)

The temptation of the ideal shades into another temptation: that of violence. When their idea of Justice does not reshape the world, the members of the Association—Mr. Munn included—try to impose their idea through force. Justice is travestied as injustice is perpetrated in its name, and humanity itself seems imperiled. When one of the night riders clubs a dog, "for an instant, the instant before the sodden impact of wood on flesh, the forms seemed to be almost merged in the darkness." (193) The Trevelyan subplot underscores the connection between violence and the ideal. Having won Trevelyan's acquittal, Mr. Munn must face the rising certainty that he has been instrumental in freeing the guilty and executing the innocent: that in the name of Justice he has committed enormous injustice. The attempt to force an idea on the world catches Mr. Munn up completely when—again in the name of Justice—he murders Trevelyan.

These, then, are the pitfalls along the path to selfhood, and,

---

4. Robert Penn Warren, "Late Subterfuge," in *Thirty-Six Poems*.

unfortunately for Mr. Munn, they constitute the forms of his life. Willie Proudfit's story of discovering the reality of selfhood, though apparently meaningless to Mr. Munn, indicates that those forms are false and unreal. They are Sartre's bad faith, Heidegger's inauthenticity.[5] They are not merely unrelated episodes, as one critic has claimed,[6] but rather represent different modes of Heidegger's falling away from the true being of integration into the dark void; they represent parts in a process of alienation from time, the world, and the self. Warren's use of the void, even at this early stage in his work, might be called existential; Heidegger's analysis of falling away in connection with inauthenticity, his observation that fallenness "has mostly the character of Being-lost in the publicness of the 'they,' "[7] describes the condition of all of Warren's lost wanderers, of whom Mr. Munn is the first.

5. Jean-Paul Sartre, *Being and Nothingness,* trans. Hazel E. Barnes, pp. 47–70. Martin Heidegger, *Being and Time,* trans. John Macquarrie and Edward Robinson, pp. 220–223.
6. Norman Kelvin, "The Failure of Robert Penn Warren," 357.
7. Heidegger, *Being and Time,* p. 220. It is clearly possible to argue that Warren is an existentialist. Speaking very loosely, one can say that anything which does not embrace Christian doctrine and indicates despair is existential; see, for example, Walter Sullivan, "The Historical Novel and the Existential Peril: Robert Penn Warren's *Band of Angels,*" *Southern Literary Journal,* 2, No. 2 (1970): 104–116. There is, in fact, a more concrete affinity in Warren's use of the void.
However, given the indefiniteness of the term *existentialism,* its application to Warren seems less useful than chic. One must discriminate among existentialisms. Warren is closest to the existentialism of Heidegger because Heidegger, unlike Sartre, advances the possibility of bridging the abyss between subject and object, of reintegrating the fragments of being into a new whole which he terms "authentic being." But even to call Warren an existentialist or a Heideggerian on this basis would seem to be straining. Heidegger has denied that he is an existentialist, and Warren, in any case, is hardly a disciple of Heidegger; there is, in Warren's novels, nothing of Heidegger's systematic analysis of Being as possibility. Warren is in all likelihood indebted to existentialism in general and to Heidegger's in particular, but that indebtedness may result from Warren's familiarity with any of a number of contemporary philosophers and theologians who to varying degrees reflect Heidegger's analysis, or it may even be no more than the sign of a common source in philosophy or the Christian pattern of conversion.

In his process of dissociation, Mr. Munn falls gradually out of time. "More and more he felt the need to protect himself by denying memory. . . . And his mind closed like a valve against all thoughts of the future." (219) Removed from the world on Willie Proudfit's farm, he muses on the fact that "the past, too, which once had seemed to him to have its meanings and its patterns, began to fall apart, act by act, incident by incident, thought by thought, each item into brutish separateness." (390) As he falls away from the true being of selfhood, time, which locates man in being, disintegrates; as he falls away from himself, he too disintegrates. He becomes, like Camus's protagonist, a stranger to himself, unable to respond to the loss of home, wife, and closest friend.

In the process of such a falling away, how does one gain the identity which selfhood involves? Willie Proudfit's story suggests that the beginning lies in an awareness, in a new way of seeing. It would seem that the man who finds himself adrift begins to find himself. The lost—the Bill Christians and Dr. MacDonalds —are blind. The seer sees unreality in the insubstantial flux of the world not through any defect in his vision, but through its accuracy. The unreality, the darkness, is there; it is the nothingness which, according to Sartre, "lies coiled in the heart of being like a worm."[8] Willie Proudfit's vision of affirmation arises out of a nearly fatal illness; this confrontation with nothingness apparently initiates his journey home to selfhood. The fact that Captain Todd's name means *death* seems to have similar implications; it is nothingness which shapes his identity.

The need for such insight into the darkness is further evident in the fact that Bill Christian and Dr. MacDonald altogether lack it. When Captain Todd predicts that some members of the Association will sell their tobacco outside of the Association, Bill Christian responds with a characteristic threat of physical violence. He does not realize that the darkness is everywhere and supposes that he will be able to demolish the occasional outcropping. He is even ready to incorporate all evil into a single tribe of men, the Sullinses. Captain Todd, on the other hand,

8. Sartre, *Being and Nothingness,* p. 21.

says, " 'Take it easy, Bill. . . . It's just human nature some of
'em will try to crawl out and sell.' " (42) Unwilling to acknowledge the void, unable to countenance the possibility of betrayal,
Bill Christian discovers darkness in the betrayal by his best
friend, Mr. Munn, with Lucille, and the discovery kills him.
Similarly, Doctor MacDonald intends to leave the region because,
as he tells Mr. Munn, " 'I might get used to the way this country
stinks.' " (358) Like Bill Christian, he supposes that the darkness can be localized and is hence conquerable or at least es-
capable. He plans to go " 'out west somewhere . . . where
people haven't caught up with themselves, yet' ": out west, to
virgin territory, from the falseness of violence to the falseness of
innocence. He seems determined not to learn that the stench
which he flees is that of Willie Proudfit's slaughtered buffalo, a
stench which reveals the inescapable presence of the dark, of the
Sartrean nothingness.

Selfhood, then, requires that one perceive the void, which
would seem easy enough, since the void appears everywhere.
Death, the many betrayals, Willie's illness, the disease of the
modern world, the various forms of falling away, are all aspects
of nothingness. Metaphorically, too, the void is everywhere. It is
the darkness in which events transpire and characters grope; it
is the sea in which everyone struggles for the substance of
reality. Thus modern life, gone out of control, is a "violent,
flooded stream." Captain Todd, the one man apart from Willie
Proudfit who seems able to withstand the flood, is "a great gray
boulder, still unsubmerged." (44) Mr. Munn, on the other
hand, first appears on a train caught in a crowd of people
surging "like a wave" (1), and much later, on Willie Proudfit's
farm, exists in his numbness at a "submarine depth" (399)
where familiar things "lost definition and merged and faltered
aqueously in the shadows." (393)

But although the flooding dark is everywhere, one cannot
easily gain the saving perception of it, for such a perception involves more than the mere awareness that darkness exists in the
world. Bill Christian and Doctor MacDonald, after all, have
such awareness, as Bill shows in speaking of the Sullinses, and
Doctor MacDonald, in telling Mr. Munn, " 'The things I've

seen done. With my own eyes.'" Doctor MacDonald goes on to say, "'It looks like those things and getting down on your knees don't belong in the same world.'" (318) The awareness which both he and Bill Christian lack is that "those things" do belong in the world. The final knowledge of the dark is that it is one with the world and a part of one's self: that the worm is *in* being.

Such is the darkness which Mr. Munn nearly sees in his snow vision of blackness, when he wonders, "Was he staring into . . . a blackness external to him and circumambient, or was he the blackness?" (109) Here Mr. Munn gains a glimpse of the nothingness which permeates being. A more stunning view, though equally tangential and unassimilated, occurs to Mr. Munn in a dream.

In the dream he saw May approaching him . . . and she held a bundle in her arms . . . wrapped in old newspaper, stained and torn. . . . The paper began to flake away. . . . He saw, then, what the paper had concealed. There, on May's outstretched arms, was a body, a foetus like those which he had seen suspended in liquid in great glass jars at the medical school at Philadelphia, ill-formed, inhuman, dripping, gray like the ones in the jars, and with a stench like death. . . . The last shreds of the sodden paper fell away from what was the face of that object in her arms. It was the face of Bunk Trevelyan . . . and somehow, he knew that it was alive and strove to speak. (395–396)

Here lies the center which Mr. Munn cannot discover to himself. At the core of time's debris (the newspaper), at the very heart of being (the foetus), is the stench of nothingness. Submerged in that dark flood ("suspended in liquid"), its face is Bunk Trevelyan's, but it is of Mr. Munn's engendering, and for him—and every man—to acknowledge. Mr. Munn, however, who, like Bunk Trevelyan is both betrayer and murderer, will not even in his dream allow Trevelyan a voice. That voice would cry complicity, and Mr. Munn chooses not to listen.

In refusing to hear of the shared darkness, Mr. Munn continues to fall away from selfhood; he chooses to follow still another false light. He sets out to kill the betrayer Tolliver and so establish one certainty: the hatred which promises to be "something he could depend on and cling to." (301) He attempts to achieve identity through murder.

Further evidence of the void confronts Mr. Munn on his mission. He spends the night in a deserted cabin which, together with the cast-off belongings within, is in slow decay. A man's jacket "had long since lost the shape of the figure it had clothed, and had stiffened earthily, once and for all, to the contour of the surface on which it had lain." (453) Completing this picture of the earthly shapelessness which lies in wait for all things human is the broken figure of Tolliver on his sickbed. Facing him, pistol in hand, Mr. Munn says, " 'You were always nothing. Nothing. Nothing.' " And of himself he says, " 'I'm nothing. . . . But when I do it, I won't be nothing.' " (456–457) Mr. Munn seems still determined to fill his emptiness with some tangible sign of his hatred.

But he cannot bring himself to shoot; he surreptitiously pockets the pistol as Matilda Tolliver enters the room and, instead of killing Tolliver, gives him a glass of water in what is a richly symbolic scene. Water here is transformed from a destructive flood into the source of life, suggesting that selfhood is not only possible amid the flood of nothingness but that the two are intimately related. While selfhood is lost in the void through the various form of falling away, the void can also give rise to selfhood. Willie Proudfit's drink signifies such renewal. Still further, an understanding of nothingness, as noted earlier, includes the awareness that it breathes into everyone. All men face the void and, to varying extents, are the void. Therefore nothingness in part defines the human community, and an understanding of nothingness would seem to mean a sense of that community, a feeling of involvement. Hence the potential significance of Mr. Munn's giving Tolliver the drink; the symbolic water is symbolically given. When, in a different scene, Mrs. Sullins refuses him a glass of water, Bill Christian quotes Matthew to her: " 'Whoever gives to drink unto one of these little ones a cup of cold water in the name of a disciple, verily I say unto you, he shall in no wise lose his reward.' " (108) Involving as it does a modern version of the wisdom which is charity, Tolliver's glass of water is Percival's Grail.

Or so it might be, if the scene in Tolliver's cabin leads Mr. Munn to understand the void. If so, he is reborn there, and his death, as suicide, is a redemptive admission of involvement and guilt. The voices of the soldiers would then seem to be the "voices of boys in the dark" because these functionaries of the chaotic world wander in a darkness which he alone sees. Insofar as it exists, however, this vision seems to be the incomplete awareness of Bill Christian and Doctor MacDonald, and the contempt implicit in viewing the soldiers as "boys in the dark" suggests Mr. Munn's continued failure to understand that he, too, is a boy in the dark.

In Tolliver's cabin there is no sign of Mr. Munn's rebirth, as he remains uncertain, will-less, and wooden. He tenders the water not of his own accord but at Tolliver's request. Matilda Tolliver, and not Mr. Munn, hears the soldiers; she suggests the direction of flight, and indirectly, the flight itself. Although in a sense he "changes his mind" in not shooting, the change seems less a shift of purpose than a loss of purpose, and a loss of purpose which he cannot quite comprehend as he puzzles, " 'I thought . . . I could do it.' " (457) His visit with Tolliver, though full of potential meaning, seems little more to Mr. Munn than another pebble on the beach of his experience, where no pebble bears a relationship to any other. It seems to teach him no more than his stay with Willie Proudfit. In analyzing alienation, Heidegger states that a man estranged from himself is driven to intense introspection resulting in a self-entanglement which precludes understanding.[9] Such self-entanglement would seem to characterize Mr. Munn and serves to explain the mental paralysis which binds him during his visit with Tolliver and his abortive escape. His mind remains entangled in its void to the very end; he raises his carefully aimed pistol and fires into the air "without thought—he did not know why." (460)

Mr. Munn never realizes that darkness becomes light, that something can be made out of nothingness. Thus Tolliver, like Willie Proudfit, has been reborn out of a severe illness, and Captain Todd has gained selfhood in withstanding a fierce Union

9. Heidegger, *Being and Time*, p. 178.

attack. Darkness has proven positive in each case, for in the jeopardy of their being they have grasped their being. The certainty of their selfhood gives their world substance, form, and meaning, as we see in the story of Willie Proudfit; Mr. Munn's world, on the other hand, even in his final view, remains a part of the dark flood as it "heaves beneath him in a long swell." (460) Nothingness for him remains negative, destructive. Appropriately, with the soldiers approaching, he thinks of the betrayal by Sylvestus, a betrayal which makes him innocent and pure, the victim of an alien world. Firing at the sky, Mr. Munn lashes out at the surrounding darkness, where the sunlight is blank, pale, empty; where even the rain is hostile. He lashes out, too, at the inner darkness, where his will lies impotent and his consciousness paralyzed. In Beckett's *Endgame,* one of the characters remarks, " 'You know what she died of, Mother Pegg? Of darkness.' "[10] Such is the fate of Mr. Munn, in his ride through endless night.

And the night does seem endless, the selfhood of Senator Tolliver, Willie Proudfit, and Captain Todd notwithstanding. In the brave new world of *Night Rider,* their certainty seems distant and unattainable. We recognize the world of the novel as our own, but these three characters seem ghosts of an earlier Southern age: a silver-tongued Senator,[11] a Civil War hero, and a fulfilled farmer. With Willie Proudfit in particular, Warren seems to be surrendering to nostalgia for that agrarian era and implying that we should return to the land.[12] The farm environment by itself is clearly not restorative, having little effect on either Mr. Munn or Sylvestus, but Willie Proudfit's integration with the land can be mistaken as the desired end. *Night Rider,* however, does make clear that the past is past and not to be regained. Willie's story is appropriately unassimilated into the narrative, for it is equally unassimilated by Mr. Munn and the

10. Samuel Beckett, *Endgame,* p. 75.

11. Bohner, *Robert Penn Warren,* p. 62.

12. Leonard Casper seems to hold something of this view; what he sees as the novel's ethical imperative is to "rededicate oneself to the painstaking, personal labor of one's fathers." *Robert Penn Warren,* p. 104.

modern world; we are left to wonder whether Willie will even be able to hold on to his farm. With the death of his son, Captain Todd's future is still more dubious than Willie's, while Senator Tolliver's sickbed may well be his deathbed.

The novel, then, leaves the reader in something of a quandary. Selfhood seems real in Captain Todd's certainty and Willie Proudfit's proud fit; it seems to begin in an awareness of the shared darkness and to end in a sense of harmony and integration. But amid the darkness with which *Night Rider* seems to shroud its modern world, is such true being attainable? There is only Senator Tolliver's rebirth to suggest that it does not depend on an irretrievable way of life, but on a way of seeing. In his subsequent novels, Warren slowly enlarges upon that possibility of vision.

CHAPTER II

At Heaven's Gate

AT HEAVEN'S GATE portrays, on a much broader canvas than does *Night Rider*, the struggle for selfhood; that struggle is won or lost by more than half a dozen characters. Three of the confirmed losers—Bogan Murdock, Slim Sarett, and Jason Sweetwater—are presented in some detail, so that their failures cast indirect light on the more successful quests. The three men share a form of false being anticipated in *Night Rider* through Mr. Munn's idea of Justice. All create grand fictions with which to organize their worlds, only to have their dreams consume them. For an example of the dehumanizing effect of the dream, we might begin with Bogan Murdock, financier and speculator, whose fiction is economic progress, a "great awakening."

We see him, in this instance, in the mind of his disenchanted wife, Dorothy, as she remembers him lying under the sunlamp:

The body was brown, an athlete's body, not old yet, modeled steelily, almost sparely, over an Egyptian delicacy of bone, the long arms almost too thin, almost painful, with their plaited perfection of muscle laid meticulously on the bone, and the chest plates of muscle knitted tightly to the bone box at the hollows, where the few black hairs sprouted crisply, like curled black wires. She could almost see it as she stood there in broad daylight—like a carved figure on a tomb, or like a dead body laid out ceremonially under that lamp. (182–183)

Bogan Murdock, we discover, is a variety of well-wrought urn. His body is "modeled steelily," his bones have "an Egyptian delicacy," his muscles have a "plaited perfection" and are "laid meticulously on the bone," his chest muscles—"plates of muscle" —are "knitted to the bone box," his hairs are "curled black wires." There is perfection in this fine façade, the perfection of a thing made. "Laid out ceremoniously" in his ritual of appearance, Bogan Murdock, like Senator Tolliver in *Night Rider*, reveals himself as fabrication. He too has built his Monclair and vaunts his mastery of life's refinements. Amid the picture of art which the passage creates, there arises a strong sense of artifice and the artificial. Dorothy thinks of him not as a man, a human being, but as a thing, an object. Just as the light of Monclair proved false, so even Bogan's sun is unreal, a sunlamp, an artifact.

Like Bogan Murdock, Slim Sarett and Sweetie Sweetwater flower in the unreal light of abstraction. Slim, like Bogan, seems in perfect possession of himself. He first appears with "one of his long white hands laid on the bar, but not for support but as in a position of control, as though it were a warrior's hand laid on a sword hilt, or a bearded mariner's hand laid, as in an old engraving, on a globe." (3) Slim's controlling idea is esthetic rather than economic, but it places him in the same world of unreality. Trying to remold his life according to his romantic conception of the poet, he invents a seafaring past, a seaman father, and a prostitute mother. Sweetwater, too, seems to be part of a very real world in his work as a Marxist labor organizer attacking Murdock's empire. But he too is warped by his idea; he will not marry Sue, whom he loves, because he sees himself as the architect of a new society who must stand outside of convention.[1]

Slim delivers the summary words on Sweetwater, on Murdock, and on himself as well when he tells Bogan, " 'You . . . represent to me the special disease of our time, the abstract passion for power, a vanity springing from an awareness of the emptiness and unreality of the self which can only attempt to become real and human by the oppression of people who manage to retain

1. John L. Longley Jr., "Self-Knowledge, the Pearl of Pus, and the Seventh Circle: The Major Themes in *At Heaven's Gate*," in *Robert Penn Warren: A Collection of Critical Essays*, ed. John L. Longley Jr., p. 71.

some shreds of reality and humanity.' " (250) Here we see more clearly defined the relationship between ideals and violence observed in *Night Rider*. The ideal begets violence, as we see there, but is begotten in a sort of violence as well—in what Slim calls "the abstract passion for power." Out of the horrified glimpse into the void comes a frenzied desire to dominate the void. In that desire for mastery, violence and the ideal are alike; the mariner, hand on globe, and the soldier, hand on sword, are one. Thus Slim is a boxer as well as a poet, and physical violence marks the confrontations between the three men: Slim faces Bogan down and is in turn trounced by Sweetwater.

In their struggle for mastery, the three men are all manipulators and destroyers. Slim and Bogan both treat men as things: Slim in his "studio" arranging relationships, and Bogan—financial manipulator—making puppets of all who venture within his sway. Dorothy, remembering Murdock under his sunlamp, gauges his essential destructiveness correctly when she envisions him as "a carved figure on a tomb" (183), a figure of death. Slim too, is such a figure, contributing to and concluding the destruction of Sue begun by Murdock. Slim is "like a subtle and courteous potentate who luxuriously entertains a friend and watches for the first affect of the poison which is in the sumptuous dish." (26) And as for Sweetwater, Sue is apparently correct when she tells him, " 'You're just like my father, you don't like him but you ought to like him. . . . You want to run everybody for their own good, and you don't give a damn for anybody . . . just yourself.' " (320)

Sweetwater, Slim, and Bogan all live various forms of falling away from selfhood; ironically, in their attempts to master nothingness they are figures of nothingness. Sweetwater partially recognizes his false being when he thinks, "Sweetie Sweetwater wasn't anything, just a name, a voice, an instrument" (308); but his recognition is incomplete because his Marxist vision of larger shaping forces leaves him untroubled by his own instrumentality. Slim, too, is nothing; Sue, talking with him, "had the feeling that she wasn't talking to anybody, that he wasn't there." (151) Bogan is nothing as well. As Duckfoot Blake tells Jerry, " 'Bogan Murdock ain't real. Bogan is a solar myth, he is a pixy, he is a poltergeist. . . . He is just something you and I thought up one night. When Bogan Murdock looks in the mirror, he don't see a thing. . . . Bogan Murdock is just a dream Bogan Murdock had, a great big wonderful dream.' " (373)

Sweetwater, Slim, and Bogan all experience twinges of malaise. Bogan, in a rare moment, confesses to Jerry, " 'If things had been different for me when I was a boy, I might—' " (21–22) The comment may well be insincere, but the very fact that he makes it seems to suggest some sense of shortcoming. Slim, in his final scene, face down on the bed of a New York hotel room "trying to think of nothing, nothing, nothing at all" (379), attempts to escape his awareness of false being. Sweetwater admits to himself that the structure of his idea may be too rigid: "He knew he had built some kind of a wall, and if he pulled out even one brick, or one stone, it would all come tumbling down. Perhaps his wall wasn't built right. Perhaps you ought to build what you believed in so you could take out a lot of bricks or stones and it would still stand up." (313) But these figures, despite their twinges of awareness, cannot be termed seekers after selfhood, for they remain caught in the unreality of their dreams.

The seekers are Sue, Jerry, Ashby, and Duckfoot. Throughout the novel, Sue is in flight from Murdock's world, whose unreality she half recognizes. "Oh what am I?" (155), she asks, seeing her own emptiness. She says to her father, " 'You don't like the people I am friends with now. You never liked them. They're— they're— . . . Real.' " (248) Her attempt to hold something real shows itself initially in her attachment to horses and later in her attachment to men. She views love as the thematic center of Shakespeare's plays and tries to make it the center of her life. By itself, however, love proves no more than the empty sexuality of Mr. Munn and Lucille Christian. As Mr. Munn discovered, love must be "a part of something else," and Sue moves from one sexual liaison to another in search of the missing element. She gives herself to Jerry, Slim, and Sweetwater, all of whom seem real; but with each of them she finds herself part of an unreal, timeless realm.[2] Sue's view of love stands revealed in its abstraction and falseness when it betrays her into murder through

2. For a discussion of timelessness in the novel, see A. L. Clements, "Theme and Reality in *At Heaven's Gate* and *All the King's Men*," p. 33.

abortion. Like Mr. Munn in *Night Rider,* like Major Murdock and Bogan Murdock, she is ready to exact life as the price for her dream.

Like Sue, Jerry Calhoun, the major figure of the novel, is in transit and first appears in flight, on "the absurd contraption of the plane."[3] Returning from New York and a completed Murdock mission, he is enjoying the glow of success and the physical comforts of the airplane cabin. "He relished that elegant resilience of the leather, the padding, the tempered steel of the plane." (7) He reviews his triumphant return to the New York hotel: "Once in his room, he had lighted another cigarette, had taken a bottle of Scotch from his bag, and had telephoned down for ice and soda. He had stood looking at the bed: the sheet creased meticulously back, the folded pajamas, the decorously plumped pillow, gleaming, which waited for the impress of his head." (8) As Jerry exults in the perfection of the airplane and hotel appointments, he proclaims his fealty to Murdock's world, the world of artifact.

Jerry does, however, experience his own sense of emptiness in this perfect, antiseptic, decorous world. He tries, in his hotel room, to break through the veneer, asking the hotel boy, " 'Are you often on night duty?' " The response is not encouraging. "The eyes which, a moment before, had seemed so anonymous, which by his inane question he had tried to stir to some warmth of personal life, now narrowed, ever so slightly, in their own self-assertion, which was cunning, appraising, vindictive." (8) The boy, too, is caught up in the sterile modern world and repulses Jerry's attempt to cut through its cold surface. "He had wanted to say to the boy, 'My name is Gerald Calhoun—Jerry Calhoun—I have something to tell you—I—' " (8) Jerry's effort to counter the sterility of his world with an assertion of personal identity and with an attempt to establish human contact must fail so long as he yearns for a place in that world, which values no human identity and honors no tie other than the cash nexus. Jerry only regains his demeanor of dignity when he reassumes his role of indifference and when he tips, as he in part realizes: "He had, with calculated deliberation, separated a bill from the others in his wallet, and had held it out." (9)

Through most of the novel, Jerry is in the process of moving slowly into Murdock's sphere. Murdock, in his worldliness, seems sure, so that Jerry adopts him as father surrogate just as Percy Munn adopted Tolliver, emulating the manner of perfection. This is Jerry's form of falling away from selfhood. He gradually learns to dress appropriately with the help of Murdock, who recommends his own tailor.[4] He enjoys the study of business and financial theory under Duckfoot because "It was so clean and sure . . . a guarantee that the world was secure, was a pattern which you could grasp and live by." (77) Deception begins to come more easily, and with it, moral deterioration. The poison at work, Jerry begins to sound like Murdock, when he talks expansively about the region's "great awakening" (130), and when, in defense of Major Murdock, he mouths the grand clichés about honor. At this point Sue leaves him, aware that the defense is symptomatic of Murdock's abstraction and inhumanity. Jerry has become a part of what Slim terms "the disease of our time"; Sue tells him, " 'You're going to be a big shot . . . it just sticks out all over you—like boils—' " (17)

The past which Jerry struggles to escape is the world which draws Sue. She meets Jerry when he comes to ride with Bogan; newly arrived in the Murdock world, he has failed to dress with the appropriate, casual elegance and chafes at his failure to remake himself in Murdock's image. Sue, however, is attracted to him because of that very failure. He has performed the reconstruction so crudely that the original shows through, and Sue, to her astonishment, sees in that original the real qualities so foreign to her father's world. She looks at Jerry as at "some kindly, awkward, humble monster which had wallowed up on the beach before her," and wonders "where, where in the world he had come from." (40)

The reality of Jerry's past continues to hold him even when he

---

4. "[Jerry's] attempt to define himself leads to a complete remolding in Bogan's image: in clothes, in speech, in attitudes." Longley, "Self-Knowledge," p. 67.

leaves it. In college, although he feels "protected from the dis-
orders and despairs of his life" by the patterns of football and
homework (52), the past continues to exert its ambivalent force.
On the one hand he feels homesick, "wanting to lie in his own
bed, on the sagging, lumpy, familiar mattress, in the dark in
that bare room upstairs where he had slept ever since he could
remember." On the other hand, he recognizes the irrationality
of that feeling, knowing that if he were to go home for a week-
end, "as soon as he got out home, with Lew and Aunt Ursula,
and even his father, he would begin to be impatient for Monday
morning." (51)

After he becomes one of "Murdock's boys," that earlier reality
continues to attract him, now through Duckfoot's family as well
as his own. When he learns that Mrs. Blake looks forward to his
visits and grows despondent when he does not come, he has "the
impulse to weep, the forgotten sensation of a swelling and
flowering, a release, within him, and coupled with that an almost desperate sense of loss and danger." (82) The "forgotten
sensation" of a "flowering" is the momentary surge of true being;
the danger is Murdock's unreal world of false being, into which
Jerry gradually drifts. The marks of his earlier being which had
so startled Sue become "worn away, smoothed out by the daily
abrasions of the world she knew, the world of Dan Morton and
her brother Ham and all the other young men like them, the
world of her father." (59)

The nature of Jerry's earlier reality, together with his ambivalent response to that reality, is preserved in the characters of
Mr. Calhoun, Uncle Lew, and Aunt Ursula. Mr. Calhoun's
salient characteristic is his bumbling,[5] which, contrasting with
Bogan Murdock's impeccable manner, underscores their polarity.
Imperfection, Warren seems to say, defines humanity, whereas
perfection refines humanity away. The novel's title is ironic;
heaven—Bogan's realm—is perfect, unreal, inhuman. We get at
least one glimpse of Jerry in the heaven of Murdock's world:

5. "[Mr. Calhoun] is complete in his humaneness, and his bumbling awkwardness and provincialism serve perhaps only to define that humanity."
Longley, "Self-Knowledge," p. 73.

After the day in the blinds, under the gray, sagging sky, beside the dead-looking, steel-colored water, the men sat in the big hall of the log lodge, before the enormous fire on the limestone hearth, glasses in their hands, their legs stretched out before them. They had removed their shooting coats and now wore jackets of soft wool or old tweed. They were, for the greater part, middle-aged or oldish men, bald, gray-haired, or streaked with gray, but in the firelight and with the flush of liquor, the flesh of these faces looked firm, ruddy, secure. . . . Jerry sat there . . . and felt that he had approached the secret focus of power and truth. (84)

Jerry's pleasure recalls Percy Munn's at Monclair, and this paradise is equally illusory, created by the flattery of firelight and the stimulus of alcohol. Against the illusion of this heaven, then, is set Mr. Calhoun's very real clumsiness, together with Uncle Lew's club foot, Aunt Ursula's blindness, and Rosemary's crippled legs. These flaws represent human limitation; they are the sign of the worm in being, of the inroads of nothingness. As such, they drive Jerry away from his family, for the dark reality of these inroads seems to deny the possibility of his heaven. But at the same time, his yearning for reality draws him toward his family, for he senses that true being depends on an acceptance of the dark. In his feelings of revulsion toward his family and Rosemary, Jerry flees from the selfhood he seeks.

Sue senses something of the relationship between the flaw and true being in feeling drawn to Rosemary, in loving the unreconstructed, bumbling Jerry Calhoun and in kissing Aunt Ursula, but, the kiss notwithstanding, in her search for love she never quite manages to embrace the flaw. She comes closest to awareness in her postoperative alcoholic revery when scenes real and imagined swirl through her mind. The abortionist saying " 'It won't hurt a bit' " is the modern world of Bogan Murdock encouraging the destruction of humanity and of self.[6] Sue in part rejects the abortionist when she sorrowfully thinks of how as a child she had lost something which she now cannot remember

---

6. "In an effort to force [Sweetwater's] hand she has an abortion, thus symbolically rejecting her last human relationship." Longley, "Self-Knowledge," p. 69.

and which we identify as the reality of her own being. But then, swinging on the trapeze, held back from the surrounding darkness by "strong hands"—Bogan's, when she was a child—she reaches—to Jerry—for a human tie in the circus world which acknowledges no human tie; her letting go is her surrender, her abortion, her death. Her falling away from selfhood is made literal as, in her dream, she plunges into the void.

Jerry, unlike Sue, moves out of unreality and towards selfhood. In prison awaiting bail, he learns of Sue's death and, unlike Mr. Munn, is not so estranged from himself that he cannot grieve. Chastened by his double loss, aware of Murdock's duplicity, he is apparently ready for a deeper awareness. At this point his father comes to prison to visit him and greets him with one word: Son. "Until that moment, the moment when the big old man said 'Son,' and again, 'Son,' Jerry Calhoun had not seen his own situation as related to anything in the world except himself. His confusion, his apathy, his grief, his bitterness . . . had been . . . almost absolute in themselves, lacking relationship even to the events and persons of the tangible world which had caused his own situation. But now, with his father's voice, his father was real." (380)

This reality, like that of the glass-of-water scene in *Night Rider,* is the reality of true being and involves the same two aspects of human solidarity and self-awareness. In his father's concern, in the assertion of relationship against the errors and vicissitudes of life, Jerry can glimpse the involvement which shapes reality. But in addition, Mr. Calhoun's reality is his awkwardness, sign of his finitude and of the void, and that reality is the beginning of self-awareness. Involvement and self-awareness together constitute the whole of true being, and this is too much reality for Jerry. Although Bogan's betrayal closes heaven's gate and makes Jerry realize that he will not be son of God, he cannot yet accept simply being son of Man. As his father approaches him he thinks, *"Oh God, if he puts his hands on me, if he touches me."* (381)

But in spite of himself, Jerry has been touched by his father. Later, in the bedroom of his father's house—a bedroom in sharp contrast to the New York hotel room—Jerry remembers a still more cruel rejection of the being which his father offers, though Jerry cannot understand the rejection as such. Thinking back to the Murdockian world he had conceived, with his father's rundown farm mentally transformed into "the old Calhoun place," Jerry realizes that his dream has eliminated Uncle Lew, Aunt Ursula, and even his father from the house. Although Jerry cannot understand that in denying his family he has rejected human frailty, involvement, and therefore the very possibility of true being, his senses lead him where his intellect cannot. Horrified at the inner void and the murder conceived therein—violence akin to that of Bogan, Slim, and Sweetwater—Jerry grasps at the glimpsed reality and envisions a new meeting with his father:

> Father, I wanted to sit by the fire, and they wouldn't be there . . . —and—and you wouldn't be there—
> Yes, son.
> I wanted you dead—I wanted you dead, father. I wanted to sit by the fire—
> Yes, son—
> You knew? Did you know?
> Yes, son.
> Oh, father—
> Yes, son— (388–389)

We suspect that this vision, like Willie Proudfit's, will come true, and, again like Willie Proudfit's, will prove redeeming. In its admission of the void ("I wanted you dead"), in its acceptance of involvement ("Oh, father—"), it indicates that Jerry has gained authentic being.[7]

A third character in search of real being, Ashby Wyndham,[8]

---

7. I am in sharp disagreement here with Longley, who seems to find little hope in the scene. He writes, "[Jerry's] hate has been turned toward Bogan, but his contempt for his father has not lessened. It will be a long process." Longley, "Self-Knowledge," p. 68.

8. The story of Ashby Wyndham appeared separately as "Statement of Ashby Wyndham." In a very brief introduction to a reprint of that story, Warren states, "The story of Ashby Wyndham is intended to have a double function in the novel. First, the story provides one of the various views

starts out in a very real farm life for which, like Jerry, he feels only contempt. Trying to escape the homestead which he shares with his brother Jacob, he beats Jacob into agreeing to sell the farm. Years later, Ashby has a vision, in which his dead son Frank instructs him to find Jacob, now become a wanderer, and take him by the hand, preaching the gospel of love during the search. Apparently some deep sense of the void in the form of his guilt pushes Ashby toward human involvement. Converted by his vision, Ashby sets out on what he takes to be his Christian mission.

As a convert, Ashby seems to stand diametrically opposite the characters of Bogan's world, who, in Ashby's words, "has got one eye cocked hot after lewdness and the other on the almighty dollar." (61) Because Ashby, with his Christian vision, seems to differ so markedly from the other characters in the novel, Warren places his story (as he does Willie Proudfit's in *Night Rider*) outside of the main narrative line. Ashby's story finally proves, however, as it merges with the main narrative, that his obsessive Christianity is one with the abstract, unreal world, to which Warren has given occasional religious overtones throughout the novel. Distraught with Sweetwater, Sue chants a mock incantation: " 'The great Sweetwater, he will defend me, he will guard me, he will throw anybody out who says boo to me, he will love me, he will cherish me, oh, his belly is a sheaf of wheat set round with lilies, he—" (355) And Jerry, in Murdock's office, "stood in the high, quiet room and stared unseeingly out the great window" (271); the office resembles a "shadowy, empty church." (268)

Ashby's religion, then, is like Murdock's, Slim's, and Sweetwater's, for it reaches toward a perfection which conflicts with

---

which are contrasted in the novel, the naive religious view at one end of the scale. Second, the story serves a purpose in the over-all organization of the plot. Ashby is driven out on his pilgrimage by two forces: by the effect, even in his remote corner of the world, of the financial speculation and corruption in the city, and by his own repentance and vision. When he finally reaches the city, he, in his innocence, brings down the house of cards which is Bogan Murdock's empire." In *Spearhead,* ed. James Laughlin, p. 415.

reality and blinds him to it. His attempt to be pure represents, in Warren's own words, "the naive religious view,"[9] and proves adequate only until it comes in contact with darkness. When the powerful Ashby receives a gratuitous pummeling and, in obedience to the Christian code, refuses to defend himself, we perceive the inadequacy of his idea and applaud when he finally loses control of himself and strikes back.

Ashby, however, remains untroubled, although the brawl pre-figures the later incident involving Pearl, which causes him considerable distress. Pearl, the converted prostitute, apparently represents human impurity, her name recalling Slim's definition of poetry as "the impurity which an active being secretes to become pure . . . the glitter of pus, richer than Ind, the monument in dung, the oyster's pearl."[10] (196) She leaves the house of prostitution only to commit murder in the name of his ideal, so that Ashby must face the horror of his proud remove from darkness and involvement.

Eventually Ashby is in part able to do so and joins Jerry in acknowledging the void. He says, " 'Lord put pore man in this world and give it him and said, it is yoren, take it and eat and know yore emptiness.' " (335) Apparently determined to know his emptiness, Ashby refuses to leave the jail. But his awareness is incomplete. Even in facing the inner darkness and thus going beyond Mr. Munn, Ashby, like Mr. Munn, remains imprisoned in his own void. In his cell he sees the nothingness of being, but not the involvement. Whereas Jerry can envision himself saying "Father" in response to his father's "Son," Ashby violates the inner promptings which sent him out to take his brother by the hand: to say "Brother" to Jacob's "Brother."[11]

The limited awareness gained by Ashby approximates the awareness with which Duckfoot Blake, a fourth seeker, begins his journey. Duckfoot sees that Murdock's heaven demands a repudi-ation of real being. Tutoring Jerry in the rules of entry to

9. *Ibid.*
10. Longley, "Self-Knowledge," p. 72.
11. I am, of course, echoing Martin Buber here. *I and Thou,* trans. Ronald Gregor Smith, 2d ed.

Murdock's kingdom, Duckfoot says, " 'All human frailty hinders and forbids. Vanity, sloth, cupidity of the flesh, false shame, and the tender promptings of our deluded nature. But you eschew the kit and caboodle.' " (73) From this ironic viewpoint, Duckfoot notes that only a hero can make the necessary repudiation. (And in fact, Bogan, Slim, and Sweetwater all have their false heroic aspects: a bringer of light via a great awakening, a poet-gladiator, and a modern Jason). Duckfoot also realizes that the unreality of such a repudiation of humanity is a reflection of the void; long after the early tutoring session, he tells Jerry that Murdock, in his unreality, looks in the mirror and finds nothing. From the beginning, Duckfoot sees the darkness within. He emphasizes his awareness of human limitation by concluding his opening tutorial with a fart: with, as he says, his "carnal envelope" richly asserting itself (74).

And yet, despite his awareness, Duckfoot falls: not by trying to master being and its void, like Bogan, Slim, or Sweetwater, but by trying to distance himself through his cynicism. He leads a life of detachment. He seems to have no friends; the only woman in his life is the prostitute he visits regularly. Like Jerry, he has eliminated his family: not with an imaginary murder, but by using the more sophisticated technique of wit and wisecrack. Thus Jerry, thinking of the Blake household, remembers Duckfoot's "high, bantering voice." (79) As the stories of Jerry and Ashby suggest, Duckfoot, in avoiding involvement, does not escape the void; his cynicism, involving as it does detachment and the disavowal of all values, is merely another form of false being. Duckfoot, then, in his flight from the world, is caught in the void of his cynicism; like Ashby, he is in a kind of prison.

When Jerry's synthetic world explodes, Duckfoot posts bail for him, but at the same time, through their developing friendship, Duckfoot is himself rescued from prison. The two help each other to discover the involvement in mankind which is one aspect of true being. Duckfoot's moment of discovery, though presumably no more valid than Jerry's, seems conscious rather than intuitive; "He knew that it mattered . . . that everything mattered. . . . He did not know how it mattered, or why, but he only knew that it did." (372–373) Duckfoot, like Jerry, is reborn.

In *At Heaven's Gate,* as in *Night Rider,* water is symbolic of modern unreality. Dorothy gives herself to the flood of nothingness as she pictures herself "shifting downward in deep water weak-green-silver-streaked bright but your eyes closed and the water breathes into you like you were a fish and you love it and it is all around you and on you and under you like hands, and that would be all if one minute could not remember the last one and didn't want the next one, didn't want anything." (186) Dorothy's daydream is a complete denial of selfhood, an unconditional surrender to unreality: a death by water.

The water also breathes into Slim. As Sweetwater, ironically aware of Slim's false being, says of Slim, " 'He swims in a lie, and he is in the lie and the lie is in him and if you could hook him and pull him out he'd hang there with his gills puffing and his eyes popping and not know what to make of it.' " (303) Slim's "studio" exists underwater: "Now and then news filtered down from that other world, like fragments shifting down uncertainly into the dim, subaqueous world." (244) And in New York, as Slim lies on his bed trying to think of nothing, "life stirred and swarmed and uncoiled in its dim, undulant, rhythmic, fulfilling roar far below, where the lights were, and while the great towers of New York heaved massively into the black sky and hedged him about." (379)

Sue is similarly caught. Significantly, she rehearses the role of Ellida in Ibsen's *Lady from the Sea,* in which Ellida frees herself from the power of "the stranger from the sea and can turn to her husband, crying out, 'Oh—after this I will never leave you!' " (96) The role has obvious relevance to Sue's life: the "stranger from the sea" is Bogan, while her "husband" is Jerry. But Sue does not see the relevance of the role; after the rehearsal she says, " 'I reckon I'm through with that silly bitch for tonight.' " Sue is, however, aware of the flood. In her apartment, "The flow and hum of the city rose and penetrated to her with a sound like the pulsation of distant surf." (208) But she comes close to escaping the flood only in her post-operative revery, when, fumbling at her childhood loss, she feels "that she was rising slowly to a surface, like a diver who had gone down deep." (359)

Jerry, too, is aware of the flood. On his introduction to Murdock's world he notices that "the individual noises of the street blurred out, here, to a steady pulsation, like the sea." (56) Later, aboard the plane bringing him back to Murdock from his New York success, Jerry pictures his world inundated; "He looked down upon the valley, and the late light, layered, striated, and rippling, was like the substance of a crystalline sea which had risen again, on the instant, to drown out that valley." (10) Finally, in jail, freeing himself from his bondage to Murdock as Duckfoot expounds on Murdock's unreality, Jerry stands "shaking himself like a big dog emerging from the water." (373)

Ashby and his disciples can maintain equilibrium only on the river. Private Porsum looks at Ashby asleep in jail "as one peers down at a bright object submerged in water, trying to make out the true character of the object through the distorting medium." (332) Sweetwater's name, in this context, is self-explanatory. Duckfoot's name is also clearly suggestive, and at least one passage underscores its relevance. When he resigns from his position in Murdock's bank, "Jerry could see him poised for an instant on the curb, attenuated, angular, his neck outthrust, his coattail jerked up above the long legs, standing there gauntly and cautiously above the rickety legs, like an aquatic fowl." (283) In leaving Murdock, Duckfoot proves himself amphibious; he has lived in Murdock's world without allowing it to claim him.

In *At Heaven's Gate,* then, Warren develops the concept of false being by making the water imagery pervasive and by closely examining several characters who live submerged in their dreams. As a result of such development, the definition of false being comes into sharper focus. *Night Rider* may erroneously be taken to suggest that the various forms of falling-away are temptations luring one against his will away from an encounter with the void and the possibility of true being. *At Heaven's Gate* makes clear that the reverse is true. As Slim tells Bogan, "the abstract passion for power" is "a vanity springing from an awareness of the emptiness and unreality of the self." (250) First comes a sense of the void, and then the attempt to master it with false being. As we have noted, out of Duckfoot's awareness

of the void comes his cynicism, an attempt to find some point of
reference at a comfortable remove from true being. Out of
Uncle Lew's awareness of the void comes his hatred, which, like
Mr. Munn's hatred for Tolliver, is an attempt to fill the void
with a certainty. Cynicism, hatred, the abstract passion for power,
the great dream, and all other forms of false being, then, do not
tempt one from the path to awareness, but are, as Heidegger
argues, attempts to flee from an awareness already glimpsed.[12]
The flight is a matter of choice; one can stop falling at any
time. When Bogan tells Jerry, " 'If things had been different for
me when I was a boy, I might—' " (22), his words are spoken in
bad faith. Like Ashby, he chooses to remain in prison. Ellida
is "redeemed from the mysterious power of the sea" when she
discovers that "the freedom of decision is her own." (96)

Through its close examination of several characters in their
struggle for selfhood, two of whom achieve it, *At Heaven's Gate*
becomes more explicit than *Night Rider* with regard to true as
well as false being. The glimpse of the void from which one flees
to false being is, potentially, self-awareness; that is, the sense that
being—one's own being as well—is the Sartrean bubble with
nothingness in the center. But such self-awareness, no matter how
complete, does not of itself mean the true being of selfhood:
witness Duckfoot at the beginning, Ashby at the end, and Uncle
Lew throughout. The examples of Jerry and Duckfoot indicate
that self-awareness comes first, but must be followed by an
awareness of others. Selfhood, then, is viewed as a fabric which
cannot be made up of oneself as a separate entity, however
fully conceived, but requires in addition a sense of relationship.

With involvement given so important a role, the question may
arise whether Warren is simply making the Christian virtue of
caritas central. Such does not seem to be the case. Lucille and
Mr. Munn in *Night Rider*, Sue in *At Heaven's Gate*, clearly
recognize the importance of love. Notwithstanding, none of the
three finds love, and it would seem that the problem is an inability to affirm any value, regardless of how clearly perceived.

12. Martin Heidegger, *Being and Time*, trans. John Macquarrie and Edward Robinson, p. 186.

Love, then, is simply not possible of itself. As Mr. Munn says in *Night Rider*, " 'Love, it's not anything . . . not when it's not a part of something else.' " (440) That "something else" is self-hood, the whole of which love is a part.

Or is it love? Duckfoot's discovery that "everything mattered" seems to suggest something broader than either *eros* or even *agape;* and if so, what is it? Duckfoot cannot explain; he knows that everything matters, but "he did not know how it mattered, or why." (373) Moreover, if selfhood is desirable, resulting, for example, in Jerry's feeling of "certainty and warmth" during his evening with Duckfoot's family, then why is it constantly fled? Is the awareness of the void so thoroughly appalling? Warren grapples with these questions in the novels which follow *At Heaven's Gate.*

CHAPTER III

All the King's Men

ALL THE KING'S MEN has its origin in Warren's play *Proud Flesh*, which was begun prior to *At Heaven's Gate*. After finishing that novel, Warren started to revise the play, but decided instead to rewrite it as a novel. Commenting, in his introduction to *All the King's Men*, on the similarity between his business-man hero, Bogan Murdock, in *At Heaven's Gate*, and the politician hero of the play, Warren says,

even some of the contrasts between them were contrasts in terms of the same thematic considerations. For example, if Bogan Murdock was supposed to embody, in one of his dimensions, the desiccating abstraction of power, to be a violator of nature, a usurer of Dante's Seventh Circle, and to try to fulfill vicariously his natural emptiness by exercising power over those around him, so the politician rises to power because of the faculty of fulfilling vicariously the secret needs of others, and in the process . . . discovers his own emptiness.[1]

Both novels present their wielders of power only indirectly, through the eyes of others. In the case of Willie Stark, however, we are allowed a searching look into the mechanism of power. The perspective is that of Jack Burden, who, as right-hand man, enjoys inside knowledge of Willie's maneuverings, and, as highly

1. Robert Penn Warren, *All the King's Men* (Modern Library edition), Introduction, p. iii.

intelligent observer,[2] offers convincing insight into Willie himself.

Thus, Jack imagines the development of Willie the Boss by picturing a strange beast imprisoned within Willie, first in embryonic form, and later, full-grown and straining to escape.[3] He pictures Willie as a boy with "a world inside himself where something was swelling and growing painfully and dully and imperceptibly like a great potato in a dark, damp cellar." (27) Again imagining Willie as a boy, Jack thinks, "Inside him something would be big and coiling slow and clotting till he would hold his breath and the blood would beat in his head with a hollow sound as though his head were a cave as big as the dark outside." (32) Later, the full-grown beast chafes under its restraint. When Willie's campaign for the governorship goes badly, Jack hears him pacing in the next-door hotel room and pictures "the feet of a heavy animal prowling and swinging back and forth with a heavy swaying head in a lock-up room, or a cage, hunting for the place to get out, not giving up and irreconcilably and savagely sure that there was going to be a loose board or bar or latch sometime." (75)

When Sadie radically revises Willie's outlook by explaining the extent to which he has been, according to her succinct analysis, "a sap," the beast is liberated, apparently through Willie's sense of impotence and outraged vanity. Under the shock of discovery, Willie withdraws, ignores the possibility of full self-awareness, and, in an alcoholic release, is projected into a realm of raw power. His false self is born. In his new guise, Willie is no longer Cousin Willie from the Country, but the Boss, with a forelock which Jack repeatedly refers to as a mane. When, much later, Willie starts to pace after flaying Byram White, Jack recalls the pacing which years before he had only heard and thinks, "Well, I was seeing it now—the lunging, taut

2. Ralph Ellison and Eugene Walter, "The Art of Fiction XVIII: Robert Penn Warren," *Paris Review*, No. 16 (Spring–Summer 1957), p. 135.

3. Warren has commented that the character of Willie Stark "gives a holiday to a part of our nature—gives it a canter." Robert Penn Warren in a letter to Leonard Casper dated August 13, 1957, quoted in Leonard Casper, *Robert Penn Warren: The Dark and Bloody Ground*, p. 122.

motion that had then been on the other side of the wall. . . .
Well, it was out of that room now. It was prowling the veldt."
(148)

What permits this beast its scope is Willie's new conviction
that the world is a jungle of corruption, a conviction which
places man beneath contempt. Friendship evaporates. The
fraternal significance of the wink to Jack in Slade's is denied;
Jack becomes a mere employee. In the jungle, men are animals
to be herded, or even objects to be moved and molded by their
maker. Sadie can say of Willie, " 'I made him.' " Willie defends
his humiliation of Byram White and his subsequent refusal to
deliver Byram for prosecution by saying, " 'My God, you talk
like Byram was human! He's a thing! . . . Hell, Byram is just
something you use.' " (144) [4] Men exist only as material, so that
this false self, animal through its origin in passion and its exclusive self-interest, is mechanical in its attitude toward others.
Thus, the Boss's voice grates, his eyeballs creak, he wheels to
the door. His pacing feet, Jack notes, "were like a machine which
was not human or animal either, and were tramping on you like
pestles or plungers in a big vat and you were the thing in the
vat. . . . The plungers didn't care about its being you, or not
being you, in the vat." (75–76)

For Willie the Boss, corruption is the sole fact of being.
When Jack makes the wishful remark that there may not be any
dirt for him to dig up in Judge Irwin's past, Willie the Boss
answers, " 'There is always something.' " For, in words which
Jack repeats several times, " 'Man is conceived in sin and born
in corruption, and passeth from the stink of the didie to the
stench of the shroud.' " "Framing" is never necessary, for "pressure" alone will serve; as Willie tells Jack, " 'You don't ever have
to frame anybody, because the truth is always sufficient.' " (358)
Giving Adam his definition of goodness, Willie says, " 'You just
make it up as you go along.' " (273–274) Animal and machine,
Willie seems to become a part of the inhuman modern world

4. Here Mr. Girault argues that Willie, in his vilification of Byram, has
the praiseworthy intent of "trying to force Byram's rebirth." Norton Girault,
"The Narrator's Mind as Symbol," p. 227.

made up of figures like Sadie Burke, with her face like a riddled plaster-of-Paris mask; Sugar-Boy, animal in his predilection for cube sugar, mechanical in his proficiency with car and gun, unable even to speak; and Tiny Duffy, who seems in his grotesque corpulence to personify all corruption, all deviation from a human norm.

Willie's sense of brute dominion becomes increasingly absolute until he views himself as all-powerful. In the hospital where Tom lies unconscious, Willie informs Lucy,

"He's all right—he's going to be all right. You understand that!"
"How is he?" she repeated.
"I told you. I told you he's going to be all right," he said in a grating voice.
"You say it," she said, "But what do the doctors say?"
". . . He's all right. Do you hear? He will be all right."
"God grant it," she said quietly.
"Grant it, grant it!" he burst out. "He's all right, right now. That boy is tough, he can take it." (397)

Here Willie confronts the world with the force of his own false being, and refuses to acknowledge any form of outside authority, medical or divine. He relies wholly on Tom's strength, which is to say, on his own; for Tom, "an S.O.B.," in Jack's words, is simply an extension of Willie the Boss.

Although the novel begins with Willie as the Boss, symbolically traveling his new highway at night in a big car driven by Sugar-Boy, we learn through flashback of his previous role, designated by Jack as "Cousin Willie from the country." In this earlier phase, Willie is not the counterpart of Bogan Murdock, but a highly idealistic innocent. In his political campaign during this phase, he holds to a high view of human nature, supposing that people will be willing to bake in the summer sun to hear his facts and figures: supposing that voters want platforms and programs. In his idealism, Cousin Willie resembles Adam Stanton, who, according to Jack, "has a picture of the world in his head, and when the world doesn't conform in any respect to the picture, wants to throw the world away." (262) Willie the Boss, on the other hand, seems intent on throwing the picture away.

Jack notes this polarity in his summary remarks. "As a student of history, Jack Burden could see that Adam Stanton, whom he came to call the man of idea, and Willie Stark, whom he came to call the man of fact, were doomed to destroy each other, just as each was doomed to try to use the other and to yearn toward and try to become the other, because each was complete with the terrible division of their age." (462) The theme of dualism is not new to Warren's thought; both *Night Rider* and *At Heaven's Gate* deal, for example, with the tension between ideals and violence. *All the King's Men,* however, provides a newly emphasized sense of internal dualism, of individual fragmentation.[5] Whereas it is important to *At Heaven's Gate* that Slim Sarett assumes the dual roles of poet and boxer, it is central to *All the King's Men* that Willie is both Cousin Willie from the country and Willie the Boss. Thus, throughout his reign as governor he is torn between idealism and brutality; after his humiliation of Byram White, he determines to build a hospital wholly uncontaminated by politics. Jack pictures Willie with alternate masks: one thin-skinned, boyish, and made of glass, the other heavy, a thing of muscle, masonry, and steel. (83) And Jack explains Willie's relationship with Tiny Duffy by concluding that "Tiny Duffy became, in a crazy kind of way, the other self of Willie Stark, and all the contempt and insult which Willie was to heap on Tiny Duffy was nothing but what one self of Willie Stark did to the other self." (105) Both selves are incomplete, the fragments of false being.

Warren's fully developed view of man's alienation from himself, together with the characterization of Willie Stark, seems to stem in large part from his work on Coleridge, which took place during the same period as his work on *All the King's Men.* In his essay on Coleridge, in fact, Warren speaks of the attempt, made by the nineteenth-century Romantics, to forge a grand philosophical synthesis and quotes words of Oliver Ward Camp-

---

5. A number of critics make this point, beginning with Robert Heilman in "Melpomene as Wallflower; or, The Reading of Tragedy," *Sewanee Review,* 55 (Winter 1947) : 154–166; reprinted in *Robert Penn Warren: A Collection of Critical Essays,* ed. John L. Longley Jr., p. 92.

bell which Jack Burden's pronouncement seems to echo: " 'The fact is that the problem was gigantic, and the men were not more than great. And they seem to have suffered all of them from a kind of divided purpose and lack of conviction, which undermined their strength: part and parcel of the duality of the age.' "[6]

In the same essay on Coleridge, Warren makes reference to *The Statesman's Manual*,[7] in which Coleridge defines man's being as a triunity made up of reason, religion, and will. True being, for Coleridge, consists of an integration of the three, for each is complete only with the other two. As a harmonious part of the triunity, reason is "knowledge of the laws of the whole considered as one," religion is "consideration of the individual as it exists in the universal," and will is "the sustaining and ministerial power" which "appears indifferently as wisdom or as love."

False being, for Coleridge as for Heidegger, involves a disintegration of the whole. Separated from its context, each part of the triunity undergoes qualitative change. Reason becomes "mere visionariness in intellect, indolence or hard-heartedness in morals." Religion, separated from the triunity of being, becomes "more earthly and servile." The withdrawn will, finally, becomes "satanic pride and rebellious self-idolatry in the relations of the spirit to itself, and remorseless despotism relatively to others; the more hopeless as the more obdurate by the subjugation of sensual impulses, by its superiority to toil and pain and pleasure; in short, by the fearful resolve to find in itself alone the one absolute motive for action, under which all other motives from within and without must be either subordinated or crushed." Further characteristics of the will in "its state of reprobation" include "hope in which there is no cheerfulness, steadfastness within and immovable resolve, with outward restlessness and whirling activity; violence with guile, temerity with cunning; and as the result of all, interminableness of object with

---

6. Robert Penn Warren, "A Poem of Pure Imagination: An Experiment in Reading," in *Selected Essays*, p. 252.

7. Warren, "Pure Imagination," *Selected Essays*, pp. 227–228.

perfect indifference of means."[8] The fallen will is, in short, the "abstract passion for power" which Slim Sarett correctly ascribes to Bogan Murdock and which is examined in Willie Stark. It is abstract, not because it is "the idea incarnate,"[9] but because, for Warren as for Coleridge, anything is abstract when removed from its context.

In Warren's fiction, the fallen will can realize itself through either world or idea. This fact explains why, in the characterization of Willie the Boss, there is a single point of divergence from Coleridge's definition of the fallen will, concerning what Coleridge calls "the subjugation of sensual impulses." Adam and Cousin Willie from the country represent the will which has idealized itself, so that *they* subjugate sensuality. Willie the Boss represents the will which has brutalized itself, in the process which Jack so graphically imagines; and therefore Willie the Boss, as representative of stark will, drinks and whores.

Whether the will chooses the sphere of world or idea, there is a resultant falling away from true being, and this similarity is more important than the difference. Both Adam and Willie try to make themselves subjects, and those around them—or beneath them—objects; both are complete in their incompleteness, and thus share in false being. In each case the will seeks an area of dominion and proves equally destructive whichever area it finds. Willie's Procrustean bed is Adam's operating table; Willie's meat ax is Adam's scalpel. Willie reduces Byram White to automaton; Adam performs his prefrontal lobectomy. While force seems to be the Boss's medium, it is Adam who kills. The brain surgeon and Jack the Ripper are indeed brothers. The asceticism of the saint and the brutality of the demagogue both seem to reflect the will to power.

Willie's path, then, is the path of the fallen will; Jack's path is that of the abnegated will. In Sadie's words, he is like "a box of spilled spaghetti." He is in flight from himself, spiritually adrift in will-lessness. An early version of this flight is the escape into innocence of his youthful romance with Anne Stanton.

8. Samuel Taylor Coleridge, *Coleridge's Works,* ed. Shedd, I: 457–459.
9. Charles Bohner, *Robert Penn Warren,* p. 69.

Anne, recognizing his attempt at escape, calls him "Jackie-Bird" and finally breaks off their romance. Two images of that innocence subsequently haunt Jack: the first, a memory of blissful drift, of Anne floating in the bay with a gull overhead, and the second, the scene in his bedroom in which he hesitated to consummate the summer's romance, struck, as he says, "by the pathos . . . of the moment which would plunge her into the full, dark stream of the world." (328) Even here, Jack has lacked the will which would have turned hesitation into refusal; he is saved from the necessity of choice by his mother's return. Jack comes no closer to selfhood for a long while; when the summer romance ends, he says, "Jackie-Bird had flown away that summer, before the fall came, to some place . . . where nobody would ever hurt him, and he had never come back." (342)

That is, other forms of flight follow, as Jack tries to redeem the lost innocence, or, if he cannot, to escape the knowledge that he cannot. One such form of false being is his career as graduate student of history; he states that he was "hiding from the present" and "took refuge in the past." (170) Marriage to Lois, an escape into sensuality, is another form of flight, while the "Great Sleep" which ends both episodes is the penultimate flight, temporarily annihilating being altogether. All of these flights are attempts at artificial innocence, so that Jack is right to call himself a brassbound Idealist, given his definition; he says, "If you are an Idealist, it does not matter what you do or what goes on around you because it isn't real anyway." (33) This flight from true being extends even into his relationship, as one of the king's men, with Anne. Waiting to meet her in Slade's, he says, "I looked up into the mirror of the bar and saw Anne Stanton come in the door. Or rather, her image came through the image of the door. For the moment I did not turn to face the reality." (255)

When reality threatens to intrude on Jack through the discovery that Anne has plunged herself into the stream of the world via an affair with Willie, Jack finds still another form of escape. He reacts to the knowledge first by fleeing west, like the young Willie Proudfit and Dr. MacDonald, in search of renewed

innocence. But he returns with a new form of flight, the protective philosophy of the "Great Twitch," according to which
"all life is but the dark heave of the blood and the twitch of the
nerve." (329) Here Jack is immersed in the world, but as victim,
and with a grand theoretical overview to explain his helplessness.
Jack chooses flight to this prison in order, in large part, to
absolve himself of blame for the affair between Anne and
Willie, or for anything else; according to the theory of the
"Great Twitch," "nothing was your fault, or anybody's fault."
(330)

In his will-lessness, then, Jack chooses neither world nor idea,
but drifts between the two. He calls himself a "brassbound
Idealist"—the term itself is a contradiction, reflecting his confusion—and has no ideals; he serves Willie Stark, but like Duckfoot Blake in his work for Bogan Murdock, holds himself
spiritually aloof from the proceedings around him. Like Duckfoot, he is in the water **but** not altogether of it.

In *All the King's Men,* water imagery is once again used to
describe the unreal flux of false being. Men of fact and men of
idea fall into the same gulf. Adam has "ice-water-blue, abstract
eyes" (109) and enters a room with the "wind off the cold sea."
(223) The curtains of Lucy's house are drawn "to give a
shadowy, aqueous light." (354) Jack, thinking of his summer
romance with Anne, remembers "the full flood of the summer."
(303) Lois is a "beautiful, luscious bivalve open and pulsing
in the glimmering deep." (322) His flight to the west he terms
"drowning westward," and says of the "Great Sleep," "I had
been sinking down in the sleep like a drowning man in water."
(288, 115) When Willie, realizing he has been duped, is about
to shed his illusions, he shakes himself "like a big dog coming
out of the wet." (84) But the sphere of corruption which he
then enters is equally fluid. Tiny has "the lightness of a
drowned, bloated body" (385), and when Sadie announces that
she is going to leave politics, Jack says, " 'You won't. You've
got a talent for this, just like a fish has for swimming.' " (395)
Willie's constituency calls for him "in a long rhythm, with a
hoarse undertone, like surf." (157) The surfaces of Willie's
prized highway "glitter and gleam like water, as though the road

were flooded." (11) We see Willie's watery dominion directly when his sycophants fall away from him "like water from the prow of a ship." (409)

All of the king's men, then, like Humpty Dumpty in the nursery rhyme of the title, sit on a wall which is the modern world of their own fabricating. That wall appears in *At Heaven's Gate* as "the great towers of New York" which, surrounding Slim Sarett, "heaved massively into the black sky and hedged him about." (379) Modern man—Humpty Dumpty—has forged his constructs to master the void; instead of providing mastery, they split his being and wall him into his own void, away from himself. To rely on the wall is to fall into the factualism and idealism which constitute false being. The fundamental antithesis of the novel, then, lies between that false being and the realism of selfhood, of true being.

To conclude of Willie the Boss that he simply falls, however, is to work injustice on the richness of his characterization and on Jack as well, for his continued interest in Willie. The title itself implies that he is more than mere demagogue. The link between Willie the Boss and the king of the nursery rhyme seems beyond question; if Humpty Dumpty is modern man, and if "all the king's horses and all the king's men / Couldn't put Humpty together again," then they have presumably tried to heal the division of our age.[10] Where do we see any such attempt made by Willie? The answer lies in his actions as governor, for he never ceases to act in the name of Justice.[11] Having failed to raise the world to the level of his ideal, he brings his ideal down

10. The title and its nursery rhyme have been variously interpreted. See, for example, James Ruoff, "Humpty Dumpty and 'All the King's Men,' " reprinted in *All the King's Men: A Critical Handbook,* ed. Maurice Beebe and Leslie A. Field, pp. 139–147.

11. Warren's own words are appropriate here: "Talos was the first avatar of my Willie Stark, and the fact that I drew that name from the 'iron groom' who, in murderous blankness, serves Justice in Spenser's *Faerie Queen* should indicate something of the line of thought and feeling that led up to that version [*Proud Flesh*] and persisted, with modifications, into the novel." Robert Penn Warren, " 'All the King's Men': The Matrix of Experience," p. 165.

into the arena of the world where he intends to force the two to coalesce. Willie's ideal, were it successfully brought down to earth, would no longer consist of abstract Truth and Justice, but of highway systems and public health plans: concrete results satisfying human needs. Thus Willie thunders to an appreciative crowd, " 'Your need is my justice.' " (278) The definition of ideals implicit in this statement is crucial; it seems to put Humpty Dumpty together again by annihilating the distinction between fact and idea.

Willie the Boss is therefore able, in Warren's words, "to fulfill, in some degree, a secret need of those about him"[12] by promising to make them whole. When Willie addresses a crowd, Jack feels "the cold grip way down in the stomach as though somebody had laid hold of something in there" (11); the hand in the form of Willie Stark enters the womb of Jack's protective idealism to force his innocence into the dark stream of the world.[13] Even Sugar-Boy responds, explaining to Jack that it felt " 'l-l-like something was gonna b-b-bust inside y-y-you." (446) Here is what Jack finally acknowledges as Willie's greatness; through the force of his being he tries to break down the walls.[14]

Willie fails, however. Sugar-Boy's wall does not "b-b-bust"; Jack feels that he "was on the verge of the truth" (346), but that truth does not appear under Willie's auspices. Force will not bring world and idea together, and Willie himself remains fragmented, with his latent idealism occasionally surfacing to torment him.[15] He fails because of his fallen will; Warren is

12. Warren, *All the King's Men* (Modern Library edition), Introduction, p. ii.

13. This point is in accord with Norton Girault's excellent discussion of rebirth imagery in the novel. Norton Girault, "The Narrator's Mind as Symbol," p. 227.

14. This is perhaps what Beekman Cottrell means by defining Willie's greatness as "a sense of personal responsibility about life." Beekman W. Cottrell, "Cass Mastern and the Awful Responsibility of Time," in *All the King's Men: A Symposium*, p. 47.

15. Elizabeth Kerr makes this point in noting that "Willie retains elements of his original high ideals." Elizabeth Kerr, "Polarity of Themes in 'All the King's Men,' " p. 33.

enough of a Christian moralist to hold that goodness cannot derive from a corrupt spirit.[16] The signs of that corruption become increasingly apparent as Willie finds in his definition of the ideal its corollary: my need is your justice. Willie's healing definition has within it the seeds of its own disintegration, for, with all needs justified, he indulges increasingly his lust for mastery; idea and fact pull apart as he comes to see in his electorate not people in need, but a contemptible aggregation contributing to the absoluteness of his power. He accuses Hugh Miller of leaving him alone to face "the other fellow's sons-of-bitches as well as my own"; Sugar-Boy speaks for Willie each time he sums up the world outside the car with " 'B-b-b-bastuds!' " In the light of such contempt it becomes clear that Willie struggles not to serve their needs but his own. His roads are a symbol of his dominion and a tribute to his capability, rather than a service to the state. And whereas his ends are signs of his power, his corrupt means, which he justifies in terms of worthy ends, simply afford the opportunity to exercise that power, as in the case of Byram White. Both means and ends, then, become functions of his need, the lust of his fallen will. When Jack's mother asks about Willie's interests, Jack is apparently correct in answering, " 'He's interested in Willie.' " (134) Some critical dispute has occurred as to whether Willie is king or Humpty; the point seems to be that he is both and does not realize it. He needs to learn that his self-indulgent abuse of others is his own wall and that, in relying on it, he too has fallen from true being.

There seems little possibility, in *All the King's Men,* of simply achieving a balance between fact and idea. Willie's failure is implicit in his attempt, and Jack's struggle also seems to suggest the impossibility of any such success as he wanders between extremes. Only once does Jack seem to reach any kind of balance. Speaking of his days with Anne Stanton after Willie's death, he says,

16. Warren writes that he was trying to portray "a man whose personal motivation had been, in one sense, idealistic, who in many ways was to serve the cause of social betterment, but who was corrupted by power, even by power exercised against corruption. That is, his means defile his ends." Warren, *All the King's Men,* Introduction, p. i.

We never talked much in those days, not because there was nothing to say but because there might be too much and if you once started you would upset the beautiful and perilous equilibrium which we had achieved. It was as though we each sat on the end of a seesaw, beautifully balanced, but not in any tidy little play yard but over God knows what blackness on a seesaw which God had rigged for us kiddies. And if either of us should lean toward the other, even a fraction of an inch, the balance would be upset and we would both go sliding off into that blackness. (429)

The seesaw may very well be balanced on Humpty-Dumpty's wall; the "beautiful and perilous equilibrium"[17] echoes the state of Ransom's Equilibrists, who seem to have no alternative to their shifting balance between fact and idea. Warren's Humpty Dumpty, however, need only discover the solution which we have seen through Willie Proudfit, Jerry Calhoun, and Duckfoot Blake: a radical conversion to true being, which will not balance fact and idea, but will rather blend them into a new whole. In this process, the fallen will redeems itself, and, in Coleridge's words, "appears indifferently as wisdom or as love."

Willie's conversion begins in a confrontation with the void over which Humpty Dumpty seesaws, when Tom has his neck broken in a football game, in part as a result of having broken training and shirked practice. Willie must face the fact that Tom has earned the disaster by being heir apparent to Willie's kingship of false being and that Willie has therefore indirectly earned the disaster too. He is left with the fact that he himself is part of the disaster and its engendering void. A resumed exchange with Lucy in the hospital indicates a change in Willie. Willie says,

"He'll be all right."
"God grant it," she replied.
He was silent for two or three minutes, still looking at her. Then he said violently, "He will be, he's got to."

17. John Crowe Ransom, "The Equilibrists," who "lie perilous and beautiful."

"God grant it," she said, and met his gaze until his eyes fell away from hers. (404)

Willie finally seems ready to bow to some force higher than his own, to admit that he is not "the Boss." Shortly thereafter Willie breaks his contract with Gummy Larson. When Tiny pleads, " 'You can't—you can't change your mind, Boss. Not now,' " Willie answers, " 'I can change a hell of a lot of things.' " (410)

Willie may be reverting to the false being of idealism at this point, but very shortly afterwards, when he has been fatally wounded by Adam (and thus confronts the ultimate void), his changed attitude toward others indicates more than a mere reversion. As "the Boss," assured of pervasive human corruption and the ubiquitous motive of self-interest, Willie has termed only Sugar-Boy his friend. His dog Buck, with rotten teeth and no apparent fondness for Willie whatever, is, Willie states, " 'the best friend I ever had. But God damn it . . . he don't smell a bit better'n the rest of 'em.' " (30) Jack, he claims, works for him only because of the nature of things, and Jack at this point would agree; explaining their relationship, Jack says, " 'He is my best pal. He hands it to me on the first of the month.' " (220) Willie's denial of any special relationship with Jack goes back to their first meeting in Slade's, through his denial of the confidential wink. But on his deathbed Willie who is no longer the Boss says, " 'I wanted to see you, Jack,' " thereby acknowledging the human tie. He does so again as he goes on to say, " 'He was OK. The Doc,' " and his words seem to accept human darkness in a new light of forgiveness. (We remember his earlier response to politicians who were using him; " 'I'll kill 'em!' ") Of his reign as governor, Willie says, " 'It might have been all different, Jack. . . . You got to believe that. . . . You got to. . . . You got to believe that.' " Here Willie seems to admit that he has not reached his potential. But furthermore, in insisting that Jack believe him, he seems to show a concern not only for what Jack will think of him, but for what will benefit Jack. In adding, " 'And it might even been different yet,' " and then correcting himself grammatically by saying, " 'If it hadn't happened, it might—have been different—even yet' " (424-425), he indicates that his rebirth has indeed occurred. Willie's language, the articulation of his being, shifts in this final statement from the intentional vulgarity of Willie the Boss to the formal harmony of true being, as Willie gains selfhood. His acts begin to form the same pattern which Brooks and Warren, in *Understanding Fiction,* ascribe to the behavior of Dravot in "The Man Who Would Be King"; "he is moving toward a sense of responsibility in power, toward a depersonalizing of power, toward pride in his people, toward a desire to bring order and peace, toward the ambition, not merely to loot and indulge his appetites, but to enter history, to achieve something worthwhile and memorable."[18]

Jack, too, comes to take his place in the pattern. He begins to emerge from his false being by learning of human limitation through Tiny. Initially, the discovery that Tiny is responsible for the deaths of Willie and Adam pleases Jack; "Duffy had done it, and that made everything clear and bright as in frosty sunshine. There, over yonder, was Tiny Duffy with his diamond ring, and over here was Jack Burden. I felt free and clean." (436) Like Willie, Jack uses Tiny as his scapegoat. But Jack's feeling of freedom and purity is shortlived, lasting only until he can, in Sadie's words, play Eagle Scout by giving Tiny a tongue-lashing. Immediately afterwards he feels exhilarated, then depressed.

It wasn't simply that I again saw myself as party to that conspiracy with Anne Stanton which had committed Willie Stark and Adam Stanton to their deaths. It was more than that. It was as though I were caught in a more monstrous conspiracy whose meaning I could not fathom. . . . It was as though in the midst of the scene Tiny Duffy had slowly and like a brother winked at me with his oyster eye and I had known he knew the nightmare truth, which was that we were twins bound together more intimately and disastrously than the poor freaks of the midway who are bound by the common stitch of flesh and gristle and the seepage of blood. We were bound together forever and I could never hate him without hating myself or love myself without loving him. (442)

18. Cleanth Brooks and Robert Penn Warren, eds., *Understanding Fiction,* 3d ed., p. 89.

The "monstrous conspiracy" concerns the community of dark-ness,[19] one aspect of the "nightmare truth" which Willie dis-covered through Tom's injury. The void is a part of being. Darkness is not merely external; the bastards are not only those outside the car.

Jack, however, cannot yet fathom the meaning of the con-spiracy, and responds to his discovery with an increased estrange-ment from being. "I hated everything and everybody and myself." (442) Jack continues to drift, and his drifting leads him to a chance encounter with Sugar-Boy in the public library. As Jack is about to tell Sugar-Boy that Duffy had killed the Boss, and so arrange Tiny's death just as Tiny had arranged Willie's, Duffy winks again. "I saw Duffy's face, large and lunar and sebaceous, nodding at me as at the covert and brotherly appreciation of a joke, and even as I opened my lips to speak the syllables of his name, he winked. He winked right at me like a brother." (445) This second wink has an effect on Jack; he does not tell Sugar-Boy about Duffy. What does the second wink tell Jack that the first wink did not? After the first wink, when Jack understands their brotherhood in darkness, he goes on to say, "We were bound together under the unwinking Eye of Eternity and by the Holy Grace of the Great Twitch whom we must all adore." (442) After the first wink, then, he still believes in the theory of the Great Twitch, according to which "nothing is your fault, or anybody's fault." But this second time, Tiny winks just as Jack himself is deciding to conspire; the wink seems to approve of his choice. With the wink, Jack is suddenly struck with the importance of choice, of will, and in the light of that importance the Great Twitch dies. Sugar-Boy confirms the importance of will, for in choosing not to kill Jack, even he is able to overcome the Great Twitch.

Jack at this point, then, has discovered the void and the significance of will—or, to put the matter differently, he has learned that man is responsible for himself. One does not reflect the darkness, but rather, creates it; one can choose to do other-wise. As Hugh Miller says, "History is blind, but man is not."

19. This kinship has been noted by John Edward Hardy in "Robert Penn Warren: The Dialectic of Self," in *Man in the Modern Novel*, p. 201.

Yet Jack goes on drifting, "still hugging the aimlessness." (448) He goes to see Lucy, perhaps thinking that full moral responsibility is to be found through her simplistic religious idealism. He finds that her idea is a dream, as she clings to the illusion that the baby is Tom's. The fragmentary pieces in the puzzle of Jack's life do not yet make up a whole.

What Jack needs, in addition to his sense of the void and of individual responsibility, is a sense of relationship, of love, of context, of matrix. The missing piece falls into place when Jack's mother tells him that she is leaving Burden's Landing and the Young Executive because of her realization that she had loved Judge Irwin all through the years. Suddenly she becomes more to Jack than a hollow creature of "famished cheeks" trying to fill her emptiness by collecting antiques and husbands. Jack can finally accept the past. Of this scene with his mother he states, "She gave me a new picture of herself, and that meant, in the end, a new picture of the world. Or rather, that new picture of herself filled in the blank space which was perhaps the center of the new picture of the world which had been given to me by many people." (458) With his new picture of the world complete, Jack can make his peace with Anne Stanton. She too has renounced the past in the knowledge that her father—" 'you think he was Jesus Christ in a black string tie' " (113), Jack has told her—has protected Judge Irwin from just prosecution. Now Jack can tell her "how if you could not accept the past and its burden there was no future, for without one there cannot be the other, and how if you could accept the past you might hope for the future, for only out of the past can you make the future." (461) Thus Jack, like Willie, like Jerry Calhoun and Duckfoot Blake, undergoes conversion and finds reality.

Similarly, Anne Stanton, Jack's mother, and the Scholarly Attorney all move toward true being. As a girl, Anne seems to show a "natural wisdom" in recognizing Jack's aimlessness and in calling him "Jackie-Bird." This wisdom, however, is no more than the ability of one false self to recognize another, just as, in *At Heaven's Gate*, Sweetwater sees Slim as living a lie, while Slim sees in Bogan the disease of our time. Anne is an idealist;

"you had the feeling that all her grace and softness was caught in the rigor of an idea." (111–112) When Jack reveals Governor Stanton's impurity, Anne responds to the void by turning to Willie, aware that he tries to make good and bad coalesce; she says to Jack, " 'You've known him all these years and you don't know him at all.' " (345) Finally Jack does know Willie, and he can become Anne's guide, introducing her to his new-found knowledge.

Jack's mother also holds herself aloof from the world, telling Jack, " 'I wish you wouldn't get mixed up in—in—things.' " She meets with her void through the death of Judge Irwin. Jack terms the "bright, beautiful, silvery soprano scream" with which she responds to that knowledge "the true cry of the buried soul which had managed, for one instant after all the years, to utter itself again." (370, 373) Discovering the emptiness of her life, she leaves her house and her husband and goes off in search of a new life, which may be real. The Scholarly Attorney confronts the void as a young man and spends most of his life fleeing from it. Overwhelmed by the duplicity of his wife and best friend, he flees to the Kingdom of Heaven, throwing the world away. Of his past he says, " 'That world and all the world was foulness.' " (216) But at the end of his life he dictates his final view to Jack: " 'The creation of evil is . . . the index of God's glory and His power. That had to be so that the creation of good might be the index of man's glory and power.' " (462–463) Thus he too succeeds in reintegrating world and idea, creating a new world of reality.

Night Rider and *At Heaven's Gate* give us glimpses of that real world, but only with *All the King's Men* is true being actually defined. We see it first in the journal of Cass Mastern. Summarizing his story, Cass writes, " 'All of these things—the death of my friend, the betrayal of Phebe, the suffering and rage and great change of the woman I had loved—all had come from my single act of sin and perfidy, as the boughs from the bole and the leaves from the bough. . . . It was as though the vibration set up in the whole fabric of the world by my act had spread infinitely and with ever increasing power and no man could know the end.' " (189) Jack as graduate student cannot find the meaning of Cass's discovery, for to him, as Jack the narrator tells us, "the world then was simply an accumulation of items, odds and ends of things, like the broken and misused and dust-shrouded things gathered in a garret. Or it was a flux of things gathered before his eyes (or behind his eyes) and one thing had nothing to do, in the end, with anything else." (201)

When the pieces of Jack's subsequent experience finally form a new picture of the world, Jack can reformulate Cass's discovery. In Jack's words, "Cass Mastern . . . learned that the world is all of one piece. He learned that the world is like an enormous spider web and if you touch it, however lightly, at any point, the vibration ripples to the remotest perimeter and the drowsy spider feels the tingle and is drowsy no more but springs out to fling the gossamer coils about you who have touched the web." (200) The spider is nothingness, a symbolic analogue of the worm coiled in the heart of being; we have seen it before in *Night Rider* and *At Heaven's Gate*. But we have not seen the reality of true being as a great web of interrelationships such that, as Jack can finally see, "the reality of an event, which is not real in itself, arises from other events which, likewise, are not real. . . . And only as we realize this do we live, for our identity is dependent upon this principle." (407) Jack seems to have discovered what Heidegger calls the "connectedness of life."[20] The web is relationship, and time is of the web, so that Jack's real being—his identity—is born with his acceptance of the past, after which he can say, "So now I, Jack Burden, live in my father's house." (462)

The biblical phrase suggests that Jack's new-found harmony may be Christian salvation.[21] Jack's response, however, to the Scholarly Attorney's final reconciliation of God and man—"I was not sure that in my own way I did believe what he had said" (463)—hardly seems the enthusiastic endorsement of the true believer. *All the King's Men* seems to indicate that, within

20. Martin Heidegger, *Being and Time,* trans. John Macquarrie and Edward Robinson, p. 425.

21. Leonard Casper states that the duty of man is "to rededicate himself to God." Casper, *Robert Penn Warren*, p. 122.

its scheme of things, the concept of God is not necessary, but is not impossible either; we can, if we wish, join the Scholarly Attorney and call the fabric of true being 'God.' In that case, the apparent contradiction between the Scholarly Attorney's early view that God is "fulness of being" and Jack's thought that "life is motion" is resolved. If God is a part of the organic web, He is immanent rather than transcendent, and therefore He changes as the web changes. But this is not the sole meaning of Jack's homecoming, any more than its meaning simply involves a return to the grace of tradition and heritage. That this latter meaning does not suffice is clear in the crime which grows out of Judge Irwin's love for a house. Burden's Landing, like Willie's father, is anachronistic, and in the end Jack must bid his farewell if he is to enter history rather than hide in it.

Jack's homecoming bears the larger meaning of the Ancient Mariner's, which, in Warren's words, is a "return to his lost unity."[22] Jack comes home to a particularly fruitful sense of man's oneness with the world. Cass Mastern writes, "If it is good, it is not lost. Nothing is ever lost." (194) After finding the dirt in Judge Irwin's past, Jack repeats the final part of Cass's statement, convinced that the taint will always surface in the end. What he finally learns is that man's good, like his evil, takes its permanent place in the world and constitutes the world: that if out of his darkness he contributes to the web of chaos, out of his awareness he can form a web of harmony. The choice and the responsibility are his. In this awareness, the will is reborn as wisdom and love. Earlier, Jack has wondered, "How can the self make a new self when the selfness which it is, is the only substance from which the new self can be made?" (373) What he learns in answer to his question is that the self is not a quantitative entity—not brain matter to be redesigned—but an inseparable part of the world's fabric, and, through the will, the shaper of that fabric: the shaper of the world, and of itself.

This analysis of Jack's new picture of the world suggests why

---

22. Robert Penn Warren, "Knowledge and the Image of Man," in *Robert Penn Warren: A Collection of Critical Essays,* ed. John L. Longley Jr., p. 241.

Warren's characters flee from true being, and why, in the puzzled words of one reader, Jack "has never seemed less vigorous, less prepared for birth than at the end of the novel."[23] Acknowledging the inner and outer void, one "owns up" to his true self; that is, one accepts responsibility for himself. Thus the theme of responsibility figures prominently in the novel, particularly after Tiny's wink. Jack must discover that the "Great Twitch" is a fiction and see that even Sugar-Boy is capable of determining his own behavior. If, however, man determines his own being, then his choices have a frightening importance. Furthermore, since his being, as Jack discovers, is contextual, the importance of the choices becomes still more frightening. To act is to touch the web, and to touch the web is to touch everyone. In the words of Sartre, "the responsibility of the for-itself [the consciousness] extends to the entire world as a peopled-world. It is precisely thus that the for-itself apprehends itself in anguish."[24] In the words of Duckfoot Blake, "everything matters," and it matters terribly; the burden of responsibility is boundless. In Jack's case, for example, it extends directly to the deaths of Willie and Adam, whom Jack has brought together, and of his father Judge Irwin, whom Jack has threatened with exposure. It is not surprising that Jack and Willie both flee from such responsibility, Jack to the will-lessness of his "Idealism" and of the "Great Twitch," and Willie to the wilfulness of stark will. Neither is it surprising that when Jack finally acknowledges the involvement which is responsibility, he sounds somewhat fearful before the "awful responsibility of Time." Since one determines his own being he must act; since the vibrations of that act spread so "no man could know the end," he can only act in fear and trembling. The need to act in such fear and trembling is precisely the Burden which Jack terms "the agony of will."

Such responsibility, although agonizing, is also liberating. Thus it enables both Willie and Jack to wrest their being from

23. Casper, *Robert Penn Warren*, p. 132.
24. Jean-Paul Sartre, *Being and Nothingness*, trans. Hazel E. Barnes, p. 556.

the flux of the unreal world. But the burden of responsibility is liberating in a more profound way. Responsibility for one's being means that one is the creator of his being, and that he is therefore free to choose what his world will be. This seems to be what Willie has learned when, on his deathbed, he tells Jack, " 'It might have been all different.' " It is this knowledge which Jack acts upon as he emerges from the study of history, where he has hidden, into the creation of history and of himself. Only from such an awareness of man's place in the world can come the goodness which is so at issue in *All the King's Men*. Through Adam and Cousin Willie, through the Scholarly Attorney and Lucy Stark, through Willie the Boss, and, in fact, through all the characters in the novel, it becomes clear that goodness simply cannot exist apart from the redemptive vision of the whole; in such isolation, goodness is a mere abstraction. The web is the whole of coherence and integrity; through false being, it falls away into the incoherence of Sugar-Boy, the dissolution of Willie the Boss, and the disintegration which, in the form of Platonic dualism, characterizes all of the inauthenticity portrayed in the novel and gives rise to the tortured idealism of Warren's next protagonist, Jeremiah Beaumont.

CHAPTER IV

World Enough and Time

THE IDEALISM which constitutes one of the concerns in Warren's first three novels becomes primary in *World Enough and Time*. Like Adam Stanton,[1] like Spenser's Artegall, who appears in the epigraph, Jeremiah Beaumont offers himself as champion of Justice—"here, thy Artegall"—to take up arms against corruption. To underscore Jeremiah's role as champion of the ideal, Warren changes the name of the original; we have not Jereboam, but Jeremiah, a prophet looking down upon corruption; not Beauchamp, but Beaumont, because Jeremiah is of the mountain rather than of the field.[2] *World Enough and Time* is, Warren informs us on the title page, a "romantic novel," and the word *romantic* is clearly being used in the pejorative sense defined by Warren in his essay "Pure and Impure Poetry."[3] Jeremiah seeks to become pure: to repudiate experience which will not conform to his conception. Unlike

---

1. Leonard Casper says, "Beaumont is Adam Stanton if Adam had survived to be brought to trial for murderously defending the image of immaculateness in a woman's honor." *Robert Penn Warren: The Dark and Bloody Ground,* p. 137.

2. The source for *World Enough and Time* is a pamphlet, published in 1826, entitled "The Confession of Jereboam Beauchamp." For Warren's use of this source, see James H. Justus, "Warren's *World Enough and Time* and Beauchamp's 'Confession.'"

3. Robert Penn Warren, "Pure and Impure Poetry," in *Selected Essays.*

Willie Stark, who tries to bring his ideal to earth in the public sphere, Jeremiah wishes to create a perfect world apart, that spoken of by the speaker in Marvell's "To His Coy Mistress," where world and time have no bounds.[4] Jeremiah must learn what Marvell's speaker already knows: that his ideal world is a dream. He must realize that the dream is conceived in what he comes to term his "vainglory of spirit"; it is the product of his fallen will.

The dissociation of world and idea begins early for Jeremiah. As a boy, he reads, on the one hand, Franklin's *Autobiography,* Love's *Surveying,* and Guthrie's *Grammar of Geography;* on the other hand, Watts's *Hymns for Children,* the Bible, and *Pilgrim's Progress.* His favorite book, the Book of the Martyrs, shows idea triumphant over world, and Jeremiah follows the lead of its heroes in rejecting the world around him, the world of his father and grandfather. After his father's death, Jeremiah notes in his journal, " 'It came to me that I would not wish to live and die thus, and that there must be another way to live and die. Therefore I searched my books for what truth might be beyond the bustle of the hour and the empty lusts of time.' " (24) Jeremiah seems to be caught between a repulsive world and an elusive ideal. But the world, though repulsive, has a certain allure for the young Jeremiah. He is fascinated by a picture, in his copy of the Book of the Martyrs, of a girl at the stake; his shifting response to her predicament is revealing. He says, " 'Sometimes the strange fancy took me that I might seize her from the flame and escape with her from all the people crowded about for her death. At other times it seemed that I might throw myself into the fire to perish with her for the very joy. And again, my heart leaping suddenly like a fish . . . I myself flung the first flaming faggot.' " (11)

The parts of his being temporarily coalesce to resolve this ambiguity through the gospel as preached by Corinthian McClardy, who seemed to make the Word become flesh, thundering that " 'God is a bear breaking the thickets of the world.' " (30)

4. Joseph Frank, "Romanticism and Reality in Robert Penn Warren," p. 248.

But the fragments come apart again through Jeremiah's blind coupling with a hag as a result of McClardy's intoxicating sermon. Further promise of resolution inheres in his apprenticeship to Cassius Fort, who, as a proponent of Relief, seeks some balance between absolute justice and human need. But Fort, encouraged by Rachel Jordan, fathers a child on her, and Jerry, manipulated by his "friend" Wilkie, chooses to see Fort's act as a worldly betrayal. He asks himself, "Where was the greatness of life? Was it only a dream? Could a man not come to some moment when, all dross and meanness of life consumed, he could live in the pure idea? If only for a moment?" (62) He leaves Fort, convinced that he must "be himself, and not be snared by the world. He had almost been snared, snared by Fort's tawdry glitter, corrupted by his promise of easy greatness, tempted to connive with the world." (68)

Turning his back on Fort and the possibility of commerce between world and idea, Jerry presents himself—"here, thy Artegall"—to Rachel Jordan, whom he has transformed into a symbol of the betrayed idea. Their minds meet, appropriately enough, over Plato's *Symposium,* as Jeremiah takes from her the book which she has been reading and reads aloud " 'how a man of high soul may use the beauties of earth as a ladder by which he mounts for the sake of higher beauties, resting at last in the single Idea of the absolute Beauty in that life which above all others a man should live to be fully man, in the contemplation of the Beauty Absolute.' " (75) In the *Confessions,* Anna, the original for Rachel, says, according to Jereboam, that she would "adore the person who would revenge her."[5] Rachel, having encouraged Fort, hardly views him as an agent of corruption; when Jerry makes the charge she says, " 'Oh, he was no villain, he was no villain. It was just . . . something that happened. . . . It was nobody's fault.' " (122) Jeremiah forces Rachel to see Fort in the light of his (Jerry's) idea, and so to demand Fort's death in the name of Justice. When Jerry is frustrated in what he calls "our great purpose" by Fort's refusal to fight, he settles into marriage and seems on the verge of happiness,

5. James H. Justus, "Beauchamp's 'Confession,' " p. 24.

with Rachel pregnant and their farm prospering. But the specter of Fort's betrayal reappears in the form of a handbill, signed by Fort, denying the rumor of his intercourse with Rachel, and attributing the fatherhood of her stillborn child to the slave Gabbo. The handbill, and Rachel's resultant miscarriage, galvanize Jerry, who blames everything on the neglect of his vow to kill Fort.

"How had he lost the mission?" he asks, and answers, "The world had taken the mission away."

> But what was the world? It was nothing. But the very nothingness was what absorbed and drew you in. And the nothingness had many faces, and many smiled. There were wealth and great place and ambition and lust of the flesh and ease. He had been saved from them . . . as easily as he had repudiated the estate of old Marcher, the tasty person of Silly Sal at Bowling Green and her kind, the patronage of Colonel Fort at the law, or the comforts of the common life. But these were not all the world.
>
> There were more insidious traps, the satisfaction of work and the turn of the seasons to show the fruit of his labor, the vanity of self-justification in his attempt to become great and prove to all men that he did not live by his wife's lands, his gratitude to Fort for favor and kindness, the labor for a general good and the justice of Relief, his joy in the love of Rachel, his hope for the future and the child. (227)

Jerry looks back at all the events of his life surrounding the vow, and sees them all "for what they were, traps, traps baited with tainted meat." (227) On Rachel's begging him not to leave for the fulfilment of his vow, Jerry sees the hag in the woods years before; Rachel herself has been only the world distracting him from his mission. He reviles that world as "enemy of the 'idea,' and of 'any truth by which a man might live, or die, who would not be the stalled ox drooling at a manger.'" (228) This total reliance on idea constitutes what Jeremiah comes in retrospect to call his first error.

Jerry's idealism is then rekindled; but with a difference. Having waited in vain during his first phase for the idea to redeem the world, Jerry enters his second phase with the conviction that the world must redeem the idea. After Rachel's miscarriage, he concludes that the idea itself is to blame for his

dereliction in abandoning the mission. " 'For,' " he writes, " 'it
is the first and last temptation, to name the idea as all, which
I did, and in that error was my arrogance, and the beginning
of my undoing and cold exile from mankind.' " (505) Though
the world has its many cunning traps, he thinks, "he never
would have taken its bait had he not taken the sweeter bait of
another trap more cunningly concealed, concealed in the 'dark
run and footway' of his own heart. And that trap was the 'idea'
—the idea itself and pure."

> It was perfectly clear. He had lived so long with the idea that that
> alone had seemed real. The world had seemed nothing. And because
> the world had seemed nothing, he had lived in the way of the world,
> feeling safe because he held the idea, pure, complete, abstract, and
> self-fulfilling. He had thought that he was redeemed by the idea, that
> sooner or later the idea would redeem his world.
> But now he knew: the world must redeem the idea. He knew now
> that the idea must take on flesh and fact not to redeem, but to be
> redeemed. (228)

Uneasy at the thought that he must kill Fort in stealth, he concludes, " 'But how could the world redeem the idea but by the
flesh and way of the natural world?' " (233) In this phase,
Jerry does not accept the world, but views its corruption as a
necessary test and proof of the idea's inviolability. He is still
trying to preserve his place apart. He writes, " 'If the idea could
not wear the dark flesh and could not keep its foot firm in the
crooked track, what was it worth, after all? I knew that that was
the last hazard, and like the bold gamester I staked all on a
card. I would submit the idea to the way of the world.' " (233)
Earlier, Jeremiah has imagined Fort's death as "self-defining
and since defining self, defining all else." (181) But the act of
murder seems to define nothing. " '*Oh, what am I?*' " (295) he
asks afterward, and, with the memory of his knife falling into
Fort, he tells himself, " 'I am Jeremiah Beaumont, I am Jeremiah Beaumont.' " (393) Despite this nagging self-doubt, as he
imagines his twisted truth undefiled by the turmoil of the legal
process, his belief that the way of the world can thus redeem
the idea sustains him. Only long afterwards can he term this

belief his second error. He writes, " 'In this thought . . . man will use the means of the natural world, and its dark ways, to gain that end he names holy by the idea, and ah! the terror of that, the terror of that.' " (505)

Jerry's third phase begins after he is convicted, as he begins to recognize the void of man's limitation. His jailer, Munn Short, recounts his experience with death: how an Indian war party had spied him making love to Sis, another man's wife, in the woods: how the Indians killed Sis and wounded him so seriously that he speaks of himself as having come back from the dead: how, upon recovery, he found himself adrift in guilt. He tells Jeremiah that " 'body dyin' " is painless, and unlike " 'the dyin what aint body . . . hit begins and hit don't stop. Till Jesus come in my heart.' " (425) Munn Short has lived with the knowledge of the void and has finally filled it with faith. Jeremiah sees in the story still more of the void than Munn Short has seen. His first response is the anger of outraged vanity, as he tells Munn Short that he does not have to hang. But then he reflects.

"I had thought of death as the absence of life, as dark is the absence of light, but it is not so. For death is a thing in itself, and has its being. As the believers say, it is with us in the midst of life. It is the mote in the ray of sunshine. It is the shadow we cast in the bright sun and moves with us. It lies beneath the blossom and is like salt in the bread on our tongue, and it is like blood in the meat we take from the skillet and the hot fire will not kill it. It rises like mist in the evening, and in the morning it lies in the bed with us and its breath stinks, and all night it was there, and I knew it. I knew that it had always been with us, even in the time of rapture and our straining for joy, and it had squatted with its painted face like a savage hid in the brush to spy upon us no matter how deep the dark and feed its lust upon our own." (427)

Jeremiah has discovered the worm in being. Absolutist that he is, having seen the reality of the void, he can no longer accept his ideal as real. " 'It was as though until that moment my way in the world had been lighted, albeit by a feeble ray, and I had known where to put the foot, but now the flame had been blown black out.' " (427)

In his resultant third phase, which, like his confrontation with the void, has been created by Warren out of whole cloth, Jeremiah submits to his conception of the world's reality. Through an escape (which Jereboam Beauchamp never enjoyed) to the swamp dominion of La Grand' Bosse, Jeremiah has ample opportunity to taste of the world. This peace is a savage parody of the innocence which he has sought throughout:[6] giving up any notion of shaping his own course, he falls into a round of drunkenness and debauchery. Later, he terms this phase his third error, stemming from the second: that is, " 'to deny the idea and its loneliness and embrace the world as all.' " (505)

Jeremiah's three phases are more similar than they are different. To summarize, he believes first that the idea will redeem the world, then that the world will redeem the idea, and third, that there is nothing but the world. The third phase is, of course, very different from the first two phases, for the idea has been discredited. But the three phases are alike in that all are forms of false being, and in all three he is equally a victim of his own dualistic vision. Still divided, in the swamp, he turns to reading the Bible (in Greek!); he regards his own being with contempt, and speaks of the peace which he finds there as the " 'black inwardness and womb of the quagmire' " (479), condemning himself by the light of his discredited idea. That idea he finds elusive and finally unreal, but the reality, though handy, seems unacceptable. Through all three of his "errors," Jeremiah maintains a rigid dualism; he remains fragmented, with the fragments cutting against each other. In that disintegration, his estate, whether nominally swamp, farm, or empyrean, is fallenness.

The minor characters of *World Enough and Time*, like those of the earlier novels, participate in the disintegration which is

---

6. In Robert Heilman's words, "the episode is a biting parody of romantic naturalism, of innocence secured in Arcadia." To Robert Berner, it is "a frightening parody of the noble savage, human perfectibility, and the Golden Age." Robert Heilman, "Tangled Web," *Sewanee Review*, 55 (January–March 1947). Reprinted in *Robert Penn Warren: A Collection of Critical Essays*, ed. John L. Longley, Jr., Robert Berner, "The Regained Past: *World Enough and Time*," p. 62.

false being. On the one hand are those who have consigned themselves to the world of fact. An example is La Grand' Bosse, the wholly unregenerate regent of the swamp, who can shrug off murder with the words, " *'c'est naturel.'* " (480) He is conceived by the narrator as the embodiment of primal darkness;[7] "respectable descendants, who did not know him and would have denied him with shame, still carried under their pink scrubbed hides . . . the mire-thick blood of his veins and the old coiling darkness of his heart." (476) With him stand his minions Lilburn and One-eye Jenkins, all bearing physical evidence of their fallenness: a hump, moss-green teeth, and a lost eye. One-eye is not quite so primal as La Grand' Bosse, but, with his imperfect vision, he is nonetheless a votary of darkness. After glutting himself on wild grapes, he appears to Jerry with "face shockingly smeared and stained, as though bruised and beaten pulpy, as though savagely painted for ritual, as though it had fed on dripping flesh and the waste blood had caked about the muzzle." (459) Sugg Lancaster, Jessup, and Bumps—as his name suggests—help to make up this particular company of false being. Their darkness is transferred to a different arena in the character Wilkie, who is in a sense a direct descendant of La Grand' Bosse, perhaps two generations removed. Wilkie's swamp is politics, and when Jeremiah discovers that Wilkie has manipulated him into Fort's murder, he asks, "What was Wilkie's face but the mask of all the world?" (501)

Equally lost in false being are those who have made the idea all. Jerry, in his first two phases, falls here, as does Rachel. When Jerry first tries to enlist in her service, she tells him, " 'I wish nothing of the world. I have put it aside and I have no place for it as it has no place for me.' " (74) She is confirmed in her rejection of the world of fact by Jeremiah, who pushes her to view Fort as villainy personified, rather than as erring humanity. " 'Dishonor's thrall,' " she comes to term him, when, in the jail cell, she joins Jeremiah on his "high and secret

---

7. Leslie Fiedler calls La Grand' Bosse "the visible shape of original sin, and the grandfather of us all." Leslie Fiedler, "On Two Frontiers," p. 742.

stage" where "poetry triumphed over dull prose and cloddish earth." (300) Another worshipper of the idea is Percival Skrogg, of whom Madison states, " 'He is wedded to justice, and will do anything for that good end.' " (323) And so, in Jeremiah's words, "Skrogg for his idea of justice had, in the end, sent Fort to my knife, and me to the rope.' " (505)

Certain characters in the novel do escape from this destructive dualism; one of these is Thomas Barron, whose portrayal puts to rest any imputation of agrarianism in Warren's early novels. As simple farmer, he follows in the footsteps of Willie Proudfit, Mr. Calhoun, and Mr. Stark. He is the end point of the impotence which grows with each of these characterizations, for he is not merely impotent, he is pitiable. Jeremiah's response to him is "a terrible, wrenching pity, and a tenderness as though he must protect the old man, at any cost, from a truth that might break on him at any moment." (154) Thomas Barron exists in a state of prelapsarian innocence; he escapes from the dualistic void because he has never even seen it. He is what Jeremiah might have become, living in uninterrupted peace on the farm with Rachel. As Warren says, discussing those of Conrad's characters who, like Barron, live happily in a simple fidelity to job, such figures "are the static image of the condition which men who are real . . . may achieve by accepting the logic of experience, but which, when earned, has a dynamic value the innocent never know." Or again, "they live in a moral limbo of unawareness."[8] Here Warren comes to final terms with whatever appeal the humble tiller of the soil may earlier have had for him.

Standing above Thomas Barron in the novel's hierarchy are those who have seen something of the dark, and who experience anguish in their struggle with false being, even if that anguish is only the wretched fear of Skrogg confronting his mortality. In his final phase, provided almost gratuitously by the narrator, the uneasy dualism of his false being evident in his name makes

---

8. Robert Penn Warren, " 'The Great Mirage': Conrad and *Nostromo*," in *Selected Essays*, p. 40.

itself fully apparent. Through the death of his first duel victim, Skrogg discovers human finitude, as he dips his fingers in the blood. In the end, he wears a vest of chain mail and barricades himself each night with an arsenal behind locked doors and boarded windows, for "in the last stage, fear had come to Percival Skrogg. . . . He had discovered that he was part of the world, after all, and that the pitiful body he wore was part of himself and precious." (94) Another postscript provided by the narrator reveals something of Wilkie Barron's saving anguish. At the height of his worldly success, like Robinson's Richard Cory, Wilkie goes home and shoots himself. Jeremiah's manuscript follows Wilkie through the years just as Cass Mastern's follows Jack Burden, and if Wilkie cannot come to terms with the reality of its indictment, neither can he continue to escape that reality. Still another of these beings in anguish is the miserable Crawford, who, having sold himself in perjury, asks to shake Jerry's hand. Jerry grants the request, saying " 'It doesn't matter' "; he understands the significance of the request only much later, when he envisions another guilty handshake.

On the highest level of the novel are those who manage to absorb that reality of darkness into the new integrity of true being. Munn Short is one of these. He has filled the void with faith: with, in his words, " 'Jesus hung on my heart lak a cowbell.' " But the very inappropriateness of the metaphor suggests that his solution is too simple-minded for those of greater intellect, like Rachel and Jeremiah. Rachel confronts the void in the swamp world of La Grand' Bosse, where she withers symbolically away; with the wisdom of insanity she yearns for a child, and involvement in life. A final confrontation with the void—the stabbing of Lilburn by One-eye and Jerry—brings her to herself, a lucidity which she announces with a scream reminiscent of Mrs. Burden's at the news of Judge Irwin's death. Thus, when Jerry accuses her of betraying him " 'when I had done all for you,' " she can answer, " 'Not for me. For yourself. You came and you used me. You made me hate Fort and you used me. Oh, I didn't hate him, I loved him, and you used me, you used me to kill him.' " (497–498) Accepting her responsibility at last, she pronounces her own judgment and kills herself in partial expiation.[9] Her last words are words of involvement and responsibility, no longer blaming but accepting blame, as she takes her place in the human communion: " 'Poor Jerry. . . . Forgive me. . . . For you—you could not—help—it—Jerry.' " (498)

Cassius Fort, the most admirable character of the novel, enters on the scene as man of sorrows, through an awareness of the dark; his is the woe of one who "knows the secrets of the world and of power, for only that man is forced to face the blankness of the last secret." (39–40) His letter to Rachel shows that, in addition to an awareness of the void, he has an awareness of responsibility. Of his " 'guilty blood' " he writes, " 'It came to guilt, not by coldness and in the calculation of man's vanity, but in hotness and folly, forgetful of the nature of things, and the debt it owed to the world.' " (147) Apparently in possession of selfhood, Fort attempts to find a political ideology which will convey his truth and heal the division of the age. First he champions the Relief Party, which, as party of the world, advocates what Jeremiah calls "justice of the belly," justice defined in terms of men's needs. (Enter Willie Stark.) Then he switches to the Anti-Relief Party, which, as party of the idea, insists that justice is a pure and inviolable absolute. These two parties are obvious reflections of man's fragmentation,[10] and Fort finds neither adequate. Jeremiah's knife, however, interrupts his next step; he "had risen in the night and gone to John Saunders' bed to wake his kinsman and say that he had a plan to " 'reconcile all in justice.' " (510) It would seem that, whereas Jeremiah places his false self on trial before a court of law, Fort places his true self truly on trial, by existence.

In confronting Rachel's charge that he has merely used her in his search for nobility, Jeremiah begins to discover the reconciliation glimpsed by Fort. The accusation shows Jerry some-

9. Charles Bohner, *Robert Penn Warren*, p. 115.
10. Warren has said, "I began to think of the political struggle of the time as a kind of mirror I could hold up to the personal story." Quoted in Casper, *Robert Penn Warren*, p. 136.

thing of his own responsibility, and his initial reaction is anger. But as Rachel dies asking forgiveness, his response shifts: "'Rachel!' The name wrenched up from some depth inside him that suddenly opened, like a wound." (498) The depth opens and the birth of the true self begins, so that Jerry can now plan a return to the human community not for pardon, but for judgment. "He had known, from the moment of Rachel's death, what he would do. . . . It was a knowledge beneath knowledge, the 'kind of knowledge that is identity.'" (502) He recognizes that Fort was "'a great man'" (503) and acknowledges his own guilt. He says, as he flees the swamp, "'Now I flee from innocence and toward my guilt, and bear my heart within me like a bleeding sore of self, as I bear the canker of my body. And if I can clasp my guilt, then both may become the marks of my triumph, as of my shame.'" (506) His will is reborn with the decision to "'shake the hangman's hand, and . . . call him my brother, at last'" (506); with that decision, Jeremiah is on the verge of ending his "cold exile from mankind" and entering the human community. He never does so, for although he sees the web of darkness (he says, "'life tells no lies in the end, for all the lies, single and particular, will all speak together in a great chorus of truth in many voices'" [506]), and although he accepts his own responsibility for the darkness ("'The crime is I'" [505]), the web of harmony ("'a great chorus of truth'") which can be created through love remains only a vision. He remains an unfulfilled seeker to the end, writing, "'There must be a way whereby the word becomes flesh. There must be a way whereby the flesh becomes word. . . . There must be a way, but I may not have it now.'" (506)

World Enough and Time explores the abstraction of idealism, the process of gaining identity, and, in general, Jack Burden's dictum concerning the fragmentation of our age. By pushing his setting back to the early nineteenth century, as in the story of Cass Mastern in *All the King's Men*, Warren indicates that the "terrible division" is not an invention of the twentieth century; by making his protagonist a rigid Platonist, Warren suggests that the source of this destructive dualism lies three

centuries before Christ in the philosophy of Plato (and Aris-
totle), where, apparently for the first time, thought is abstracted
from experience, and the perfect man described as the man of
reason. It is here that the psychic seed is split, giving rise to the
incompleteness of modern man, whether in the form of the
"pragmatic" Willie Stark or the "romantic" Jeremiah Beaumont.

In its investigation of that split, *World Enough and Time*
deals in part with existential absurdity: the disparity between
man's rage for order and the incoherence of the world. Seeking
"the nobleness of life," (which he would hardly view in terms
of man's rage for order), Jeremiah lives what the narrator
terms his "dream." But the narrator is a modern figure and
calls our attention to the absurdity, noting that Jeremiah prepared a drama for himself which "was to be grand, with noble
gestures and swelling periods, serious as blood," but which
went somehow awry. "At times even he, the hero, forgot his
lines. At times it all was only a farce . . . with its comic parody
of greatness. . . . To us, at this distance . . . it is sometimes
the most serious speeches and grand effects which give the farce.
And by the same token, we may find the pathos in those
moments when the big speeches are fluffed or the gestures forgotten, when the actor improvises like a lout, when he suffers
nakedly from the giggles and the inimical eyes, or flees from
the stage." (5) Both farce and pathos derive, as the narrator
realizes, from the discrepancy between world and idea; both are
aspects of absurdity.

But the narrator is not altogether reliable;[11] he does not see
that the absurdity is not insurmountable, so that he insists on
the primacy of the dream. He theorizes, "It may be that a man
cannot live unless he prepares a drama, at least cannot live as
a human being against the ruck of the world." (5) But Willie
Stark on his deathbed is no longer preparing a drama, nor is

11. Leonard Casper has suspicions to this effect, and speaks of "the his-
torian's professional blindness" and "passionless quest for fact." Casper,
Warren, p. 148.

Jack Burden in his last phase. And although it may be argued that Jeremiah prepares a drama even in his final recorded intent of going to " 'shake the hangman's hand, and . . . call him my brother, at last' " (506), the possibility exists, if the narrator is not altogether reliable, that Jeremiah gives up even that drama at the end. Thus, he is not "surprised" in camp by One-eye. (How could the narrator know? His inside source of information, Jeremiah's journal, has concluded.) Rather, Jeremiah has presumably given himself up to One-eye, as Mr. Munn in *Night Rider* gives himself up to the soldiers, and so has finally come down from his stage. He would hardly resist One-eye, having determined to return to the hangman.[12]

The narrator, a contemporary, despises the modern world, as he indicates with his cynical diatribe near the very end, in which he sounds much like the unregenerate Duckfoot Blake or Jack Burden. As a part of the dualistic world of false being he ranges from that cynicism to an idealism which, both in tone and content, is indistinguishable from Jeremiah's. It is the narrator, for example, who terms Rachel 'Hecuba' (Priam's wife, most chaste of women), and asks, "Who is Hecuba, who is she, that all the swains adore her? She is whatever we must adore. Or if we adore nothing, she is what we must act as if we adored. . . . And if we do not adore her, we can adore nothing or only Silly Sal, who was found tasty in Bowling Green by the hot boys of the town." (128–129) Here the narrator shows himself split by "the terrible division of our age"; he is undramatized and unidentified because he lacks " 'the kind of knowledge that is identity.' " He sees his world's dissociation and absurdity, but he does not see the possible reintegration of selfhood, and so cannot properly construe Jerry's end. Thus he himself ends,

12. Perhaps relevant to the conception of Jeremiah's demise is the ending of Dravot in the story "The Man Who Would Be King," according to the analysis of Brooks and Warren. Dravot, the king, is beheaded and his head brought back in a bag. Brooks and Warren note that he has insisted on dying with dignity, and conclude that "when external kingship is lost, internal kingship is achieved." Cleanth Brooks and Robert Penn Warren, eds., *Understanding Fiction*, 3d ed., p. 56.

not with a conclusion, but with a question, which indeed suggests *de te, fabula,*[13] but also reflects his own unawareness.

After *All the King's Men,* where the nervous, modern rhythms of Jack Burden play against the ornate rhythms of Cass Mastern, why has Warren fashioned a modern narrator who seems so indistinguishable from his Cass Mastern-like subject, Jeremiah Beaumont? It would seem that since the age, with its "terrible division," includes both nineteenth and twentieth centuries, Warren has chosen to cast his story with a single rhythm, tone, and frame of consciousness in order to reflect the unchanging dilemma which that division poses. The narrator and his subject merge in their quest for rebirth, and their narrative becomes the spiritual autobiography of the age.

13. Robert Heilman, "Tangled Web," p. 109.

CHAPTER V

Band of Angels

IN AMANTHA STARR, heroine of *Band of Angels* and Warren's first female protagonist, Warren traces the negative path away from true being. Whereas Willie Stark loses himself in force, and Jeremiah in the light of his ideal, Manty seems to lack even the strength necessary for such loss. Hers is the will in abdication, which has appeared previously in the characterizations of Percy Munn, Jerry Calhoun, and Jack Burden. Like Jack in his "Great Twitch" phase, Manty sees herself as victim of the world's chaos, which she seeks to escape by finding her strength in others. They are the angels of the title, who seem to promise her identity; the most important of these are Hamish Bond, Rau-Ru, and Tobias Sears.

Bond, perhaps the most compelling character in the novel, begins his career with a descent into the world of darkness. His mother, we learn, has dreamed of slave-holding, aristocratic origins, and posits as summum bonum a respectability which she defines in those terms. Bond reaches manhood when he cuts through her lie and exposes it, even as he remains caught up in it. As he leaves home he says to her, " 'Yes, I'm going away, but if you're so nigger-crazy, I'll fix you. I'll go where there's a million niggers. . . . I'll wallow in niggers. I'll be ass-deep in niggers. And then . . . and then you'll be satisfied.' " (182) Slave-holding respectability is her ideal; Bond sets out to destroy this ideal by obtaining slaves through violence, by immersing himself in the dark reality of the world.

But with his disappearance into the African darkness he succeeds only in substituting a new form of false being for the old. Telling Manty how he had participated in plundering an African village for slave-booty, he says,

"It was like a dream. It was like a dream you had long back, but didn't know you had had until suddenly, now you remember it, and the dream is coming true . . . just like, deep inside you, you had known it would. Known without exactly knowing, that is.

I said: *This is not me.*

I said: *They drove me to it.*

I saw the picture of my mother's face in my head, that last day, and I said: *I reckon you are satisfied now.*" (197)

Bond's response to the picture in his mind is one of mingled satisfaction, revulsion, and hatred. Satisfaction, because he has once again exposed his mother's illusion; revulsion, because he has committed an outrage against humanity; hatred, because he has committed this outrage in reaction to his mother, and therefore hatred because she has managed to maintain indirect control over him. In reacting to the idea he serves the idea, and thus he does not remember his mother, but sees "the picture of my mother's face in my head." In his revulsion, he saves the child Rau-Ru from death, but only after the world has left its mark: a crippled leg. That leg, sign of human imperfection, is the potential light amid darkness, but Bond does not acknowledge it; Manty notes much later that he swings up into the barouche not like a crippled man, but "with the lightness of youth." (324)

As long as he ignores the crippled leg, Bond is caught in unreality; having rejected the world's nightmare as well as his mother's illusion, he embarks on a new course which proves no more real than they. He tries to be Prince of Light instead of Prince of Darkness, cloistering himself behind a wall and an alias, and visiting the world with kindness. But the kindness which he brings is "kindness like a disease" because it is kindness without a real basis, kindness without a heart, kindness which, in ignoring the real self, can only torment. The name "Bond" indicates the real basis which he seeks and cannot find, arising as it does only through acknowledgement of limitation, of the crippledness which he denies. He plans to introduce such a bond by marrying a "respectable" Creole girl, but driven by motives which he cannot explain, he violates and then rejects her. Of the violation he tells Manty, " 'I was cold as arithmetic, and I did it like I was doing sums. It was something it looked like I had to do, to wind up some business. It was like a revenge. But I don't know for what. She had never done anything to me.' " (201) The violation is a revenge taken against his mother, for he is still under her control. He cannot form the bond which he seeks because to do so, he thinks, would be to accept her respectability.[1] Trapped between that respectability and the nightmare of the world, seeking an escape through Manty, Bond can only watch as the nightmare intrudes on the artificial island of his false being. That intrusion takes the form of the Civil War and "Beast" Butler; it takes the form of age, which Bond views as a fall from the purity of youth into the corruption of the world. He admits to Manty that he fought with the man about to "examine" her on the auction block as well as, later, with Charles Prieur-Denis, not out of kindness, but to test the extent of his fall. Manty seems to offer a momentary stay against confusion. Bond yearns toward her not because he loves her but because she is "so little, and young," and he sees her as the innocence which will redeem his age. When Manty asks why he bought her, he answers, " 'I felt old. My leg got to hurting.' " (202) Both age and ache, which might have signalled limitation and led Bond to see and accept Manty, only serve to remind him of his fall, and he can see Manty only as the saving innocence. He remains trapped within the walls of his own fabrication, and tells Manty, " 'You know . . . about everything I ever set out

1. Speaking in an interview of Bond's relationship with his mother, Warren has said that Bond "gets away from her by making the lie come true, but true in some shocking not respectable way that would violate her need for respectability." Robert Penn Warren, "The Art of Fiction XVIII: Robert Penn Warren," *Paris Review*, 4 (Spring–Summer 1957), reprinted in *Robert Penn Warren: A Collection of Critical Essays*, ed. John L. Longley Jr., p. 39.

to do, I've done. I got everything I ever set out to get. And you know, it was always just like something getting tighter and tighter around me.' " (164)

Bond's escape is death. Standing before Rau-Ru's band with his head in the noose, he sees Manty and laughs. Apostle of purity and abstraction, he sees rising around and against him the world's blackness, which he had earlier embraced, first as destroyer and then as protector; he laughs at his own prophecy —"ass-deep in niggers"—come perversely true. The world's blackness seems to have destroyed him, as well as his mother. Viewing himself as victim of the world, he leaps from it into death. Manty says, "It was strange, the way he jumped, not like a crippled man, but with a force and lightness . . . like a young man leaping, but the leap was an old man's leap, out from the old angers . . . into the stunning blaze of release, into the apocalyptic pain, into quietness." (324) Even in the end he does not acknowledge his crippledness. His leap is an escape from the world, as is his "crazy laughing," which "seemed to blow the whole world away in a gay, demoniac gust." (323) But although Bond's death is an escape, it is an escape without honor, for the burden is to be borne, the crippled leg accepted. Bond seems to discover the true path when he proposes to Manty, but she denies him this path, and, as the epigraph states, only through death can he be rid of the wrong his father did.

The pattern of fathers and sons is repeated in the relationship between Bond and Rau-Ru, the Negro whom Bond saved as an infant from the African village holocaust and who has been raised "like a son." Bond, defining for Manty Rau-Ru's status as *k'la,* says, " 'It's almost like a brother or son or something. . . . A *k'la,* he's sort of like a part of you. He's sort of like another self.' " (200) And when Rau-Ru makes his first appearance, Bond "slapped Rau-Ru's left shoulder in the immemorial gesture of fatherly affection." (119)

Rau-Ru, however, discovering that white man's justice does not extend to him when he saves Manty from Charles and is whipped prior to trial, rejects Bond and the white world. When Manty tells him that she favors Negro suffrage but that there must be no *coup d'état,* he says, " 'You talk funny . . . for the

little nigger Old Man Bond flattened out. . . . Was that how
you learned about white folks' justice that you like it so well?' "
(275–276) But Rau-Ru discards more than "white folks' justice."
He tells Manty, " 'It wasn't Mr. Lincoln who set me free. . . .
It was you. . . . Oh, yes, if it had not been for you, I might
have been there yet. Ass-kissing Old Bond. Oh, yes, I was the
k'la—I was the *k'la!*' And he swung his right hand out in a
sweeping gesture of revulsion." (270–271) Affection itself becomes contemptible to him, a sign of his own subvervience to
whiteness. Like the young Hamish Bond, like La Grand' Bosse,
he creates a dominion in the quagmire, as leader of a band of
swamp outlaws.

From here, Rau-Ru follows a crooked path. He reappears
under Tobias's wing in a new guise, as Lt. Oliver Cromwell
Jones, his name proclaiming his determination to impose pure
idea upon the common world of fact. Torn between Dr. Dostie,
who advocates freedom through violence, and Tobias, who seeks
freedom through legal channels, Rau-Ru chooses legality until
Tobias goes secretly to secure the arrest of all the dissension
leaders in order to avert bloodshed. Feeling betrayed, Rau-Ru
chooses his black cap over his white and goes out into the storm
of the world, which leads him back to the swamp. Jimmee says,
as he takes Manty to the old swamp hide-out, " 'All dat time
. . . and hit's been waiten . . . lak hit knowed we'd come
back.' " (316) Betrayed by Tobias, betrayed by the soldiers who
failed to come and aid in the fight, Rau-Ru sets out to confront
the original betrayer, Hamish Bond, whose justice had proven
false. When Bond, head in noose, commits suicide, Rau-Ru
tells Manty, " 'I might never have done it.' " As he realizes, he
is torn between his outrage and his love, and, paralyzed by
Hamish's death, he lies waiting for the bushwhackers and his
own death.

The pattern of fathers and sons repeats itself still again in the
relationship between Leonidas and Tobias Sears. Leonidas is a
friend of Emerson—the older Emerson, quite clearly—who has
reached a comfortable accommodation with the world. Tobias,
whose name in Greek means "God's goodness," is a version of
the young Emerson, and, early in their courtship gives Manty a

copy of Emerson's essays. His idealism involves a contempt for the world; he speaks of "the filthiness of things," and says, " 'It's so hard right in the middle of things to remember that the power of soul must work through matter.' " (238) His idealism is a flight from that world and from his father; when, feeling trapped by the worldly Col. Morgan, he abruptly announces his plan to work in the Freedman's Bureau, Manty thinks, "And so he had . . . seized on that idea, that very instant, as the escape, the escape from both, from the Colonel, from father. And I suddenly had some vision of Tobias straining to break out of something, straining to rise from something, a clinging mass, undefined, gray, viscous." (260)

With the inevitable failure of his idealism, Tobias moves toward worldliness. He cannot impose his idea upon the world because that world is the object of his contempt, merely the matter through which "the power of soul must work." His dedication to the cause of emancipation seems no better than the attempt to preserve the idea of himself as savior. When the attempt falters in the chaos following emancipation, Tobias seems to draw closer to a true awareness. He says, talking to Manty of Emerson, " 'He speaks of a spirit above our heads that contradicts all we say. Now Emerson meant a spirit better than we. But I tell you he had things reversed. . . . We said fine things . . . and a spirit sat over our heads and contradicted all. . . . Oh, Manty, we undertook to do good in the world, but we had not purged our own soul.' " (294) Tobias is led by such doubts toward a cynical acceptance of the worldly market-place, and that acceptance hardens when he is disinherited as a result of his attack, in his book *The Great Betrayal*, on "thing-ism," on the world of his father Leonidas. Of the disinheritance and its effect Manty says, "How subtly by that repudiation, had old Sears drawn Tobias from me and delivered him into the hands of that exigent goddess: Success. . . . And so Tobias, even as he sat behind the closed door of his study anatomizing the evils of our time, became himself the child of the time." (347) At the end of this phase, the noble Tobias, become seducer and drunkard, finds his version of Rau-Ru's swamp and Hamish Bond's jungle.

Manty, like her angels, Hamish, Tobias, and Rau-Ru, exists as a part of what Tobias calls "the falling motion of the world." (263) She, too, is in recoil from the corruption of the world. As a child, she had been sheltered from the storm of the world by her father, who had, at one point, literally taken her in from a thunderstorm. But, in failing to sign her manumission papers, he has turned her out into that storm and has left her to discover her origins only at his death: to discover that that storm is elemental and attacks through the very blood. In *Band of Angels,* Warren has found his most telling theme for assimilating the void into the new integrity of true being. In order to come to terms with herself, Manty must acknowledge her own "black blood," which she views as the void, human limitation, corruption. She says, for example, "I saw myself, the stain of the black blood swelling through my veins . . . a flood darkening through all the arteries and veins of my body—no, a stain spreading in a glass of clear water." (227–228) In her flight from corruption and selfhood, she casts herself as victim of a meaningless and inexorable process. She pictures an enormous devouring plant of the jungle—African, significantly enough—and says, "I knew myself the victim, the insect, the animal, struggling . . . against the constriction of the great gullet of time, caught in that corolla of history." (309) As "Amantha," with its Latin root of "lover," she is lover of purity, of "Starr-ness" (one thinks of Sir Philip Sidney's 'Astrophil,' with its Greek root and identical meaning and function) ; but she is also a more earth-bound lover in that, like Sue Murdock, she seeks union with those who seem to promise safety from the world's devouring process.

Manty is drawn to Hamish Bond because he seems to embody the idea of kindness; he has, she is told, "kindness like a disease." It is that kindness with which he has tried to create and illumine his place apart from the world. She gives herself to him after he has rescued her from a storm, just as her father had done years before. Happy with Hamish in his place apart, she thinks, "Whatever the world was like, away off yonder . . . all that world was beyond *Pointe du Loup.* I could not bear to hear about it." (146) But *Pointe du Loup* means Wolf's Point; when Hamish unmasks himself and reveals his past, his island dissolves, and Manty is left to confront the world and its void. She says, "I hung on to Hamish's hand, tighter, and tried not to think what he was saying. If I thought too much about that, I didn't know whose hand it was, and I felt that if I let that hand go, I would slip off the edge of something and go falling." (189) Manty feels herself about to fall into her own blackness. She says that, after Bond's confession, she "would lie in the dark," and in that darkness of her mind, the taking of New Orleans by "Beast" Butler, the rampaging mob, Bond's ravaging of the African village, his violation of her upon concluding his story, would all coalesce into a picture of vileness triumphant, leaving her "filled with my shivering shame and defilement." (214)

Manty is drawn to Tobias because she sees him as conqueror and savior. He too rescues her from the storm of the world when he intervenes and puts an end to the corporal's attack. While Tobias is away, she thinks, "He would come again, step down from the golden mist, high-faced and smiling from his victorious cloud, and save me." (251) She sees Tobias, in his pure Emersonian idealism, as a statue in white marble (237, 239), and, caressing him, feels "the darkness behind my tight-shut eyes, yearning toward an image, the brilliant whiteness, the beautiful whiteness, of that image that overhung my mind like a bright cloud." (241) "What had the past to do with me? Nothing, I told myself, and believed it." (234)

But as events threaten to entangle Tobias he flees from them and from Manty, leaving her to ask, "Oh, why did the world intrude?" (257) When Tobias, having learned of her "black blood," abruptly breaks off love-making to pursue his Freedman's League concerns, Manty experiences a painful sense of rejection. Wondering why he has fled, she asks herself, "In revulsion from a taint in my blood, in fear of the dark passion of my blood . . . in answer to a noble obligation, in desire for some truth which was not in me to give or understand?" (344–345) She views his flight as an escape from the taint of her blackness into the purity of his idea, and feels confirmed in her view as she contemplates his framed poem and its opening words, "I who, alone." "All at once I knew that I had never had a share in Tobias's poems. No, for their hero of the hundred

names . . . had been Tobias dying from me, dying in per-
petual, self-perpetuating flight from me, dying in a constantly
re-enacted suicide and infidelity . . . dying always into . . . the
nobility of Truth, dying into the undefiled whiteness of some
self-image." (345–346) Excluded from the "bright cloud" of
Tobias's ideal, Manty flees to Rau-Ru, who has also rescued her
from the world's storm, saving her from rape. She views Rau-Ru
as the blackness of the world, and, when she finds him, asks to
see his scars, which she imagines as looking like oakbark; she
joins him in his swamp.

What Manty seeks from her three angels, is, first, freedom. At
the outset of her narrative, she says that she used to think, "If
I could only be free." (3) Happy with Tobias, she thinks, "It
was not old Hamish Bond who had set me free. No, it was
Tobias Sears who had done that. His own clarity and freedom
had made me free. Free from everything in the world." (234)
But Hamish Bond seems to prove himself a part of the world,
and Tobias refuses to lift her into his cloud. In Rau-Ru, Manty
seeks a different kind of freedom, the freedom which she thinks
of during the orgiastic cotton-burning in New Orleans. She
thinks, "So this, too, was part of what the music and cheers, a
year ago, had promised. Perhaps this was the deepest and
dearest promise, the most secret—the brute communal roar, the
dancing, the flames leaping in darkness. Perhaps this was the
fulfillment, the freedom, that all the lifting hearts had really
yearned to." (174) But Rau-Ru proves no freer than Manty,
as, stricken, he lies awaiting the arrival of the bushwhackers.

Manty also seeks identity from her three angels. "Oh Who
am I?" (3) , she asks, opening her narrative. A nagging sense of
her own nothingness pursues her. Thus, she does not tell Hamish
Bond about her father, "For to tell would be to admit that he
had prized me as nothing, that I was nothing." (149) When
Hamish Bond reveals his past, he suddenly becomes real to
Manty, and she thinks, "I had known Hamish Bond for a long
time, and I guess he had been nothing but a bulk. . . . He had
not been real, just a dream I was having, a dream I had to have
and cling to." (163) This thought is frightening to her, for "If
Hamish Bond had been nothing but a dream I was having, this

was like finding out, of a sudden, that I myself was nothing but a dream which he had been having, and had to have for his own need. So I was nothing, and alone in the middle of nothing. It was the feeling of that old nightmare of mine, of being in the middle of a desert and the horizon fleeing away in all directions." (163) When Tobias flees her bed, Manty again feels reduced to nothing. She notes, "And then came the chillingest thought of all. Not his reason for flight from me . . . but his reason for coming to me in the first place. . . . I had been nothing to Tobias Sears, nothing at all, nothing but the excuse for his magnanimity. Oh, my life was nothing." (345) Such, too, is her life when she returns to Tobias after her episode with Rau-Ru. She describes their life as being "like a picture—life frozen in quietness, in eternal stasis, out of time, no past, no future, no beat of the heart." (340)

Manty's mistake lies in conceiving of freedom as an escape from blackness, an escape from self. In that conception she is as divided as Jeremiah Beaumont: as divided as Miss Idell and Seth, who shift between the sensual and the saintly. What Manty comes to learn is that freedom results from an acceptance of blackness, for both freedom and identity have their source in an acceptance of the void.[2] Rau-Ru, taunting her about being a nigger, is leading her in the right direction, but she repudiates him as well as her own necessary self-awareness, when she blurts out to the bushwhackers, " 'I'm not nigger, I'm not nigger—I'm white, and he made me come—oh, he made me!' " (332)

Since she has cast Rau-Ru as symbol of darkness, it is in the form of Rau-Ru that that darkness returns to haunt her imagination, to hound her. When a broken old Negro appears, she takes him to be Rau-Ru, "pursuing me all those miles and years, like an old hound sniffing devotedly on that cold and fading scent." She gives him money, "as though by thrusting into that gray-palmed, twisted, clawlike old hand whatever bits of metal

2. Charles Bohner remarks the black-white polarity, but by interpreting the poles in terms of "primitivism and civilization, slavery and freedom, ignorance and knowledge," he seems to miss the point. Charles Bohner, *Robert Penn Warren*, p. 133.

or stained paper I had, I could buy something, absolution, oblivion, knowledge, meaning, identity." (355) With that memory, Manty suddenly comes to terms with her blackness. "I said the word *nigger* out loud, several times. You know, I had not thought about that for years. I simply hadn't." (355)

Having acknowledged her blackness, Manty is ready to understand freedom. When the old Negro dies, she thinks at first that his death has somehow freed her from the past and her betrayal to the bushwhackers. But doubts nag at her, until, keeping vigil beside the grave of the old Negro, she despairingly thinks, *"Nobody can set you free,"* and finds herself adding almost involuntarily, "except yourself." (363–364) Here the relevance of the Civil War background is particularly acute: the Yankees are no more a band of angels than are Manty's saviors. Manty's thoughts continue:

Except yourself, except yourself: and that thought meant that I had to live and know that I was not the little Manty—oh, poor, dear, sweet little Manty—who had suffered and to whom things happened, to whom all the world had happened, with all its sweet injustice. Oh, no, that thought, by implying a will in me, implied that I had been involved in the very cause of the world, and whatever had happened corresponded in some crazy way with what was in me, and even if I didn't cause it, it somehow conformed to my will, and then somehow it could be said that I did cause it, and if it had not been for me then nothing would ever have happened as it happened, Hamish Bond would never have plunged from his cotton bale, Rau-Ru would never have waited in the ruined house while Jimmee pleaded with him to leave, Tobias would never have become the sad, sardonic slave of bottle and bitterness, the betrayer of women, and the thought of my involvement in all things was awful. (364)

Earlier, conceiving of herself as victim, Manty has been in fundamental agreement with Hamish Bond who, when justifying his African carnage, says, " 'I didn't make this world and make 'em drink blood. I didn't make myself and I can't help what I am doing.' "[3] (189) At the graveside Manty discovers that she has indeed made herself, and that she has been a victim

3. Robert Penn Warren, "The Art of Fiction XVIII," p. 38.

only of the world which she has made. She realizes that she has
been enslaved by her own constructs and enthralled by those
who seemed to embody the positive side of those constructs.
When Tobias later calls her "poor little Manty," she responds,
" 'Don't ever call me poor little Manty again!' " (375) Thus
Manty discovers her will; she discovers that she has full responsibility for herself in her limitation and for others in theirs.
That discovery means identity and freedom as well, for such
responsibility, involving as it does "the sweet possibility of
being," is the only real freedom. The theme of freedom, inter-
related as it is with the theme of identity, is present in all of
Warren's novels, and is made explicit as early as *At Heaven's
Gate,* in which Ibsen's Ellida is redeemed from the sea of false
being when she discovers that the freedom of decision is her own.

Tobias enters the world of true being through Mr. Lounberry, while Manty's entry is made complete. As Tobias champions Mr. Lounberry's cause and helps him wash down long-
lost father Lounberry alias Old Slop the garbage man, Mr.
Lounberry's cause becomes Tobias's, and Tobias, too, comes to
terms with blackness by assuming a responsibility for it in
which he himself is at stake. He too redeems the vile and garbage-
ridden past with the ritual bathing. After Tobias has told her
the story, Manty thinks with "a dry, gnawing envy of Mr.
Lounberry, who could honor his father," who had rejected him.
"With that I felt some relaxing in my soul. Maybe that could
be learned, if I tried. Maybe Mr. Lounberry could teach me, if
I tried. Then, all at once, like catching the glint of a piece of
thistledown drifting in high sunlight, I knew that my father
had loved me." (373) Through that realization, the past becomes
acceptable for Manty as for Jack Burden, and she too can take
her place in time.

With Tobias and Manty both having gained selfhood, *Band
of Angels* ends by celebrating their new found communion.
When Tobias says, "darling, darling, darling," he echoes Manty's
earlier words. She had thought, "I shall not be able to . . . say
darling, darling, darling, till he can believe my voice and heart,
and believe that there is no success and no failure, just the sweet
possibility of being, of defining ourselves as ourselves, together

beyond loneliness in some charity deeper than what is love because it is the dark depth of the fountain from which love leaps but as the flashing spray." (353)

Earlier, Manty has found love impossible in the presence of blackness; when she succeeds in calling her never-seen mother's face to mind, she notes, "my heart gushed with joy: *oh, she loved me!*' Then suddenly, I thought, *'but she was a nigger.'* The face was gone." (74–75) Finally, however, she realizes that the acceptance of blackness does not preclude love, but rather, makes love possible. For love can only exist in the world of true being, which depends on the freedom of responsibility and the acceptance of blackness which is the starting point of that responsibility.

Manty's angels are caught in the same struggle of false being as she; they too cannot accept blackness. They have all come to terms with it—Hamish as Protector, Tobias as Redeemer, and Rau-Ru as Champion—but their terms are false, for all hold it in contempt. Hamish's attitude is clear in his repeated words, "Ass-deep in niggers." Tobias views blackness as part of the viscous mass pulling him down; he tells Manty, " 'Those damned niggers better fight.' " (242) And Rau-Ru, sharing Manty's self-hatred, declares that he is a radical only because of his skin, "and stabbed a forefinger brutally into the flesh of his own cheek." (274) In *Band of Angels* Warren draws the racial problem within the sphere of his metaphysic. It becomes clear that the whites, in their hatred, have projected their own dark void onto the blacks, so that the blacks are their Tiny Duffys; the blacks, in their self-hatred, cannot break away from that projection. But the novel is 'racial' only in a secondary sense. Warren's primary reason for using the metaphor of blackness seems to be to enlarge upon his statement on the disease of our age: to show that, in their hatred and self-hatred, blacks and whites find refuge from responsibility in their intellectual constructs.

Another aspect of that flight from responsibility is introduced through the words of the epigraph: "When shall I be dead and rid of the wrong my father did?" The fathers have sinned by passing on to their sons both the blackness and the constructs which make that blackness loathsome. The sons take refuge from any blame by hating the fathers, just as they do by hating blackness. They must discover, if they can, that the sins of the fathers and the sins of the sons are one and the same, that all struggle together in the dualistic sea of false being. This is particularly clear in the case of Hamish Bond, seen as spiritual father of Rau-Ru. It is also clear in Manty's realization that her father did not sign her manumission papers because, caught in his love and his own idea, he could not bear to acknowledge, or even to face, her blackness. As in Warren's earlier novels, the binding constructs crumble, the voluntary enslavement ends, with the realization that darkness is inherent in being, and that, as in the case of the crippled Hamish Bond, the defect is the man. Without that realization, all perch separately on Humpty Dumpty's wall.

CHAPTER VI

The Cave

THE CAVE, like all of Warren's previous novels, deals with people who have enslaved themselves, although their enslavement once again takes the form of domination rather than prostration. Like *At Heaven's Gate* and *Band of Angels, The Cave* develops its theme through several major characters of nearly equal importance. Of these, the central figure is perhaps that of Jack Harrick, and particularly the young Jack Harrick as he exists in memory. Early in the novel we learn "what the old ones, dreaming back, said about him." "For thirty years Old Jack had dragged jugs dry, whipped his box till folks fell down from dancing, cracking jaws with his fist like hickory nuts under a claw hammer, and torn off drawers like a high wind in October stripping a sycamore to bare-ass white, all over Kobeck County, counties adjacent and contiguous, and other points of the compass." (13) Jack's wife, Celia, has somewhat similar recollections of Young Jack:

a tall man standing in the back of the truck, riding the sway like a sailor on a tossing deck, hatless, wearing a red-plaid mackinaw and cowhide boots, waving a rifle easy as a bookkeeper waves a lead pencil, yelling like a kid to some crony, yelling: "Yeah, got two!" then tossing the rifle down, on a tarpaulin-covered heap in the trunk, and leaning over to come up with a fresh bearskin, holding the big head high above his own head, the bear-jaw open in a last white-tusk-studded rage, the eyes staring, fixed and unrelenting under the blood-streaked spot where the 30.30 had gone in, the big hide, fur-side and blood-side, trailing down half over the red mackinaw, and the man's face, with a blood-streak now on it from the hide, grinning with teeth as white as the bear's. (160)

Young, tall, strong, self-assured, washed in the blood of the bear "with teeth as white as the bear's," Young Jack seems to be a natural force, the conqueror of both society and nature. As such he is a legend in his time.

But the fate of the bear is not irrelevant; Young Jack, for all of his apparent freedom, is trapped. His anguish reveals itself through a flashback to his courtship of Celia. Holding her hand during an evening promenade, "he found himself sucking in his guts tighter and tighter and wasn't even sure he felt the soft sod under his feet. Then clear as a bell, a voice seemed to say in his head: *I'm not ever going to die.*" (144) His initial response to the voice in his head is exhilaration at his prospective im-mortality, but "perfect joy" gives way to fear. "Suddenly, he didn't know whose hand it was he held. That was the terror. It was like waking up in the dark and not knowing who you are." (144) He desperately reaches out for something real and pro-poses to Celia.

But the anguish of his unreality persists even in marriage. In his love-making, he does not call Celia by name. The danger, the narrator informs us, is not that Jack will mistake the name of the woman in bed with him. Rather, "the danger was in the fact that Jack Harrick might not know that Jack Harrick was there, might not, in fact, know who Jack Harrick was, or if Jack Har-rick had ever existed." (148)

We realize eventually that the false being in which he struggles is his own legend. On the one hand, it terrifies him with its void, for in it, he glimpses "the vertigo of his own non-being." (387) On the other hand, when fatherhood threatens to bring him into the real world of birth and death, he flees to Chattanooga, where, in his words, " 'I was drunk for three weeks, and I lay around with whores in alleys and hotels and whorehouses.' " (300) This flight, as a last attempt to be true to his legend, is not altogether successful; in his words again, " 'I lay drunk on the floor, and I fought cops, and I got my head busted and got put in jail and got the clapp.' " (300)

This ignominious ending prefigures the dwindled role of Old Jack, who, dying in his symbolic wheelchair, paralyzed by his dilemma, is still caught, like so many of Warren's protagonists, in his inability to reconcile dream and reality. He remembers his proposal to Celia as his original sin, the betrayal of his legend, and thinks, "if then, that instant, long back on the mountain, he had turned and seized her, not falling on his knees, and ripped her, and ripped out of her what he wanted, and flung her aside on the grass and run on over the mountain, his feet scarcely touching the rocks as he ran under the dark, barely star-teased sky, then nothing would ever have happened like this. All would be different, he would not be dying in a wheelchair. He would have run on forever, over the mountain, under the dark sky." (151) Had he been true to his idea, he thinks, he would have made good his escape from the world, so that mortality itself would have been outdistanced. Instead, he proposed to Celia, and that proposal was a fatal violation of the pure idea. Caught up in his Paul Bunyan dream, Old Jack cannot take the pain-killing pills prescribed, because to do so would be to admit that he is not a legend but a man, and as such, a part of time and subject to decay.

Jasper, Celia, and Monty are also caught in the legend of Jack Harrick. Jasper seems "a chip off the old block" to Monty, and to old Jim Duckett as well. (19) But although we never see Jasper directly, we learn enough about him to know that he finds the legend considerably less congenial than does Young Jack. Jasper, for example, is strangely affected by his talks with Jack; both Monty and Celia remember that Jasper came away from those sessions, in Monty's words, " 'not looking like himself, sort of streaked and white in the face.' " (23) And Celia, recalling with distaste the bawdy jokes with which Jack regaled Jasper, remembers that Jasper began to avoid the house; " 'That was the time when things were worst . . . the tales about his carryings on and disappearings.' " (240) Jasper, it would seem, finds the legend a difficult legacy. He cannot be true both to his inheritance and to himself. His "carryings on" are his attempt to wear the proffered mask and mantle; his "disappearings" are his attempt to escape the dilemma. Celia has another memory of Jasper which further attests to his predicament. She remembers an angry exchange with him which concludes with his "looking down at her in the strangest way, as if he wanted to say something to her, to tell her something, cry out to her." (241) This is Jasper's moment of anguish, the counterpart of Jack's moment of terror on the mountain; both father and son reach out to Celia.

She, however, cannot respond to their appeals, because she too is caught in Jack's legend. When she first sees him holding up the bearskin on the pickup truck, "waving his rifle easy as a book-keeper waves a lead pencil" (160), she is apparently impressed by the contrast between this bear-god and the bookkeeper, between the vital Jack Harrick and her sickly father. When her companion remarks, " 'He's a blacksmith,' " Celia's response is revealing. "For a moment Celia Hornby didn't quite connect the remark with the man on the pickup truck. It didn't seem, some-how, that that man had ever had to earn any living, in any way, just flashing through the world, holding up a bloody bearskin, and yelling in good humor and joy." (162) She is enthralled with Jack as the image of a vitality which she dissociates from the mundane reality of labor.

Even in marriage, Celia remains exhilarated by this image; in his blacksmith shop, she "always felt caught in a thrill of strange-ness tinged with guilt, in adventure about to be divulged, in an enchantment." (294) When Jack says, as she embraces him in the shop, " 'Gosh, Baby—and me all dirty, like I am,' " her re-sponse is to "let her arms go loose . . . feeling some dullness of the world over her, some weight of encroaching time and sad-ness. (294) She feels "a sense of defraudment" as his comment destroys the dream and returns her to the world.

Monty, like Jasper and Celia, is also a victim of Jack's legend. He views Jasper as "a chip off the old block," and tries, perhaps too literally, to follow in his footsteps by wearing the same boots. At the same time, Monty suspects that his self-consciousness and sensitivity set him considerably apart from Jack and Jasper, and he sees the void of his false self. When Old Jim Duckett asks,

" 'Air you a chip off the old block?' " Monty nods weakly, but "he knew he wasn't. . . . He didn't know what he was. He was nothing." (14) Monty tries to create himself in the image of Jack and Jasper, knowing that he cannot; he can only chafe at the control which that image exerts. When Jo-Lea compliments him on his guitar-playing and asks, " 'Did Jasper teach you?' " Monty's response is, " 'Any fool can pick something out of a box.' " (29)

The four Harricks, then, are trapped in the legend of Jack Harrick; trapped in their separate dreams are Nicholas Papa-doupalous, Isaac Sumpter, and MacCarland Sumpter. Nick's dream is an adolescent fantasy appropriate to his undeveloped mentality: a fantasy of Jean Harlow, now dead, but alive in Nick's mind as his blond, swivel-hipped darling. As he watches the artiste Giselle Fontaine perform, clothed only in the night club's haze of cigarette smoke, her bleached hair whipping about, his fantasy comes momentarily to life. Giselle Fontaine and Jean Harlow merge "in the stunning, shattering, noiseless collision of the dimension of Time and non-Time, Dream and non-Dream, which is what we call Truth with a Capital *T*." (43) "What was going on to the throb of the tom-tom, swathed in blue cigarette smoke out there on the patch of floor . . . seemed like the projection of the fantasy which had underlain, under-propped, all life. The two things were one thing, and its name was joy." (51)

Nick marries Giselle Fontaine, and with his eyes resolutely closed during their love-making, attempts to wed world and idea. "But the two things—the fantasy and the real woman named Giselle Fontaine—started to fall apart." (51)

The impromptu drama, the ritual, the squinched eyes, never quite accomplished . . . what they were supposed to—that is, the fusion, the identification, of the dream and the actuality. Either the thing didn't work at all, and all he had a grip on was the actuality which some nagging something deep in him said wasn't so damned different from other actualities that he had to be in such a mess about it. Or the thing worked too well, and with his eyes squinched tight, he clasped the expensive, swivel-built dream with the breath of honey and his name on her tongue, and he was unfaithful to Giselle and his moment of vision in the honky-tonk.

Anyway, whichever way it went, he was bound to feel bad afterwards. There was bound to be an infidelity and the anguish of remorse. (52)

Such is the predicament of Nick, caught, too, between the dream of Jean Harlow–Giselle Fontaine and the reality of Sarah Pumfret, tubercular and going to fat: the one unattainable, the other unacceptable.

Ikey is also caught up in false being, and its shifting forms constitute a reminder that false being is a flight from selfhood. Initially, he dreams of academic achievement. "If the grade came right, if there was the A, he felt an icy joy that, for the moment, justified all. If the grade was not an A, he received the information with an equally icy detachment, but under that icy surface he would begin to feel a slow coil and dark eddying and would know that in a few hours he would fall through into that black despair. . . . And then out of that blankness would come a new, grimmer energy." (101) For Ikey as for Slim Sarett in *At Heaven's Gate,* academic achievement seems no more than an index of the power sought to fill his emptiness.

Ikey's second phase, his relationship with Rachel Goldstein, is ambivalent in its possibilities, as the narrator indicates by saying, "it was as though he had entered a dream. Or, perhaps, had left the dream and, at last, entered reality." (111) It is for Ikey to determine whether the relationship will be one of love or mere sexuality. In his desire for power, he chooses to view the relationship in bad faith. He feels "a sense of entrapment, a sense of weakness, a sense that he was paying a price for something, for the red Mercedes . . . for the tail he got. . . . he had sold out and he was paying the piper and he wasn't calling the tune. It was a hell of a price to pay for tail." (125) Thus Ikey in his need for power disregards the saving possibilities of the relationship and twists it into a thing of unreality.

Ikey's final phase consists of manipulation refined into a profession. Ikey finds his life's work in Johntown, when he coldly capitalizes on the misfortune of his partner Jasper. As Ikey engi-

neers the news coverage from the mouth of the cave and maneu-
vers Jebb Holloway—like Jim Duckett, a voice of the world—
about, Ikey has a disquieting thought: *"How am I different from
that turd?"* In answering that question, Ikey finds his full justi-
fication and definition: "Jebb Holloway had done only and
exactly what he, Isaac Sumpter, had determined. Jebb Holloway
hung at the end of a piece of string, and was therefore a thing.
Isaac Sumpter pulled the string and was, therefore, a man."
(279) But as Ikey drives from Johntown to Nashville, a deepening anguish follows him. Seeing activity in a farmhouse, he
imagines the real life within, and "felt some dry entrapment of
the heart, a clutch of terror and despair." (366) Confirmed, however, in his false life, he flees to the airplane, the symbol of unreality (as in *At Heaven's Gate*) ; and "all things behind sank,
at that withdrawal, into their undifferentiated sleep of nothingness and the darkness of unreality." (366)

Ikey flees, like Slim Sarett, to the unreal city, where, despite
the opportunity to manipulate others on a grand scale as an
executive with the mass media, his anguish continues to haunt
him. He last appears replete with techniques of forgetfulness:
"Success and Seconal were readily available to him, the most
famous product of Scotland was still in long supply for the ex-
port trade, and the caravan of Eastern beauties, to the faint
servile clink of small gold chains, came footing slowly toward
him, with humble yearning in their eyes, over the golden sands
of the desert waste." (372) His passion is for power, so that he
has, not *affaires de coeur,* but rather, a captive harem. Rachel,
whom he had earlier distanced by calling "Goldie," he now de-
humanizes still further by thinking of as "the Jew Girl." Infected
with his fatal indifference, she marries a short eight months after
his infidelity only to die in childbirth; her husband, *"the* Gorham
Blumhof,"* is a member of a New York brokerage firm, an ad-
junct of the unreal city. Here in the wasteland, with expanded
powers of destruction, Ikey reigns, "the great Ikey," "totally himself." (372) Reality would mean being simultaneously more and
less than himself, in his commitment to others. His completeness
is the completeness defined by Jack Burden in *All the King's
Men,* when he notes that Adam and Willie were each complete

with the terrible division of their age; it is the completeness which Monty calls "the lonely nothingness of being only yourself."

Ikey's father, MacCarland, is also caught, trapped in his conception of the Christian ideal; Celia reflects that MacCarland "tried as hard as any man she had even known to walk as Christ would have him walk." (154) But MacCarland has indirectly contributed to his son's downfall. Ikey is correct in likening his father to Abraham, ready to sacrifice a son for an idea. The potential savagery of righteousness becomes evident when MacCarland confesses to Jack, " 'I wanted your son to die. Because . . . it was your son.' " (381) Jasper represents Jack's legend, and, worshipping one idea, MacCarland cannot tolerate the existence of another.

The Harricks, Nick, Ikey, and MacCarland all give themselves over to dreams, then, and the marks of their allegiance (which define all of Warren's lost) are constant. First, and most generally, a certain malaise results. MacCarland tells Jack, " 'I am in such distress. . . . I know that I sin against God in questioning His will, but it is true.' " (178) Jack and Jasper have their moments of terror and yearning, while Ikey, fleeing Johntown, feels his "clutch of terror and despair." (366) And Nick, the narrator informs us, suffers constantly; "in that deep, dark, angry, secret center of his being tears fell without ceasing." (42)

Second, and more specifically, their existence takes place and seems to take place outside of time. Thus, Jack's moment of terror follows a fleeting sense of immortality, and, much later, he wonders at his change from young boy to old man. Similarly, Nick thinks, "It looked like it was not right for a man to live a long time and wind up somewhere and not even know how he ever got there." (361) Ikey, fleeing to his plane, "was worrying about time." (366) Giselle Fontaine "was descended, *though she did not know it,* from a long line of learned New England divines and talented Pequot-killers." (43, [italics mine]) And Timothy Bingham, caught in his position and respectability, "thought of the future only when forced to do so to calculate interest, and thought of the past, resolutely, not at all." (37)

Third, an uncertain identity results from the commitment to illusion. Celia, remembering Jack's Chattanooga escapade as a betrayal, thinks that it was "as though those [subsequent] years had meant nothing, and therefore her life nothing." (306) Monty Harrick is "a chip off the old block" who knows that he is not a chip off the old block, suspects that he is nothing, and blames Jo-Lea for not valuing the athletic prowess by which he defines himself. Jack is "Old Jack" to Johntown, "John T." to Celia, "Jumping Jack" to his army buddies; he is left with the familiar question in Warren's novels of "Who am I?" Sarah Pumfret is Giselle Fontaine; Isaac Sumpter is Isaac, Ikey-Baby, and Ikey; and Nicholas Papadoupolous is Nick Pappy, saying, " 'They got things they call you. Like Nick Pappy. But if it is not your right name, it looks like sometime you don't know who you are, maybe.' " (304)

Fourth, the characters lost in their dreams try to fill the void with some form of domination, some assertion of the fallen will. Jack's legend is the result of such a lifelong attempt, and even Old Jack, about to gain self-definition, is momentarily satisfied with the memory of a physical triumph: "The fellow was broke and bleeding and any self-respecting undertaker would have refused the job." (386) Ikey flaunts his intellect and later feels the need to lord his triumph over Jim Haworth. Monty wears boots like Jasper's and a rakish hat; Nick drives a yellow Cadillac convertible. The commitment to the unreality of false being results in a callousness toward others, based on the tacit understanding that they too have no reality. To Ikey, Rachel is "the Jew-Girl," and Jim Haworth is "that bastard Haworth." To Giselle Fontaine, Nick is "the crud." Nick, in turn, cares not at all about the real Sarah Pumfret, and during his tight-eyed sexual performance "she felt like she wasn't there." (51) Monty cares for Jo-Lea, yet views her as a score to be chalked up. And Jack, recalling his courtship of Celia and the moment of terror, thinks, "Yes, he hadn't cared what even she had wanted or needed, what emptiness she had to fill to be herself." (387)

Ikey finally succumbs to his dream, but most of the novel's major characters fight their way out of the void and enter the real world. Jack comes to awareness as he absorbs the fact of

Jasper's death. Trying to find himself, Jack has to go back in time to a scene in his childhood, where he prepares for his mother the lie which is the beginning of his persona: "Then, so suddenly he thought he might burst into tears . . . he realized that he could not remember how that little boy with the wet hair had turned into him, into the old man who was going to die." (377) Here he begins to see that his life has been a lie, and that there was been no time between boyhood and old age. He has simply not existed.

Looking farther into the blackness, he realizes that, as he admits to MacCarland, " 'I wanted my son to die' " (381), and that he desired that death in fear of his own. As he plumbs the void of that fear, he moves toward an awareness of his own limitation. In what is perhaps the most important passage of *The Cave,* he muses,

> But who was Jack Harrick?
> And he thought that he, the old man sitting under the electric bulb in the bare room, sweating in the wheel chair, could not possibly be Jack Harrick.
> No—for Jack Harrick, he knew then, was nothing but a dream. He was a dream dreamed up from the weakness of people. Since peo-people were weak, they dreamed up a dream of their need for violence, for strength, for freedom. Sitting there, he hated them for their weakness, for all their praise and envy, for the hands clawing at him for his strength, or in supplication for it. Old Jim Duckett, patting and clawing. . . .
> He hated them for their weakness, which had made him what he was.
> No, he knew then, as calmly and indifferently as morning mist parting on the mountain, the weakness was not theirs. It was his. Out of his own weakness, he had dreamed the dream of Jack Harrick. And from that, all had followed. (388)

Jack realizes that he is not the hero but the victim of his legend, and that, as such, he is the victim of his self-conception. The scene is resonant because, like the storm scene in *King Lear,* it depicts the archetypal discovery of self. Jack, like Lear, learns that he has reigned in a kingdom of illusion, and finds "the thing itself: unaccommodated man."[1] His answer to his repeated question "But who was he?" like Lear's "I am a very foolish fond old man,"[2] is eloquent in its simple humility: *"I am an old, nigh-illiterate, broke-down blacksmith, sitting here in the middle of the night, and my boy is dead."* (388) Thus Jack finally confronts the stench of the inner void. "He was wondering if there was a stink. Perhaps there was some he could not smell. Because it was his." (389)

Having gained self-awareness, Jack is ready to understand involvement. Initially, as he examines the guitar, he cannot correlate three facts which occur to him: *"It was my box. . . . It was Jasper's box. . . . It is Monty's box. . . .* They were like three strings vibrating together, and he strained to catch the melding sound, but could not." (400) One last thought momentarily holds him back from the responsibility melding the separate strings into a harmony which, in another image, is the great web of being. This thought is that all men are like him, and that he is therefore not to blame for anything. But with the recognition that he and Monty differ comes the sense of responsibility which marks Jack's entrance into the real world. His song indicates his new love for Jasper, together with his new acceptance of death; he sings, " 'I'm coming, son, I'm coming, take your Pappy's hand.' " (402) The three strings sound their harmony in this song and, shortly following, in "a big clanging chord," after which he says, " 'I don't want to bust the box. . . . It's Monty's box.' " (403) As he says, to the sound of that chord, " 'Let that anvil ring!' " (403) we realize, with Jack, that death and the void form part of life's harmony.

Celia and Monty also break out of the unreality which is Jack's legend. Celia realizes that the legend has shaped Jasper and driven him away. She tells Jack, " 'That's why he kept staying away from home. . . . That's why he crawled in the ground. To get away from everything. To get away from the

1. William Shakespeare, *King Lear*, III, iv.
2. Shakespeare, *Lear*, IV, vii.

hands on him. . . . To get away from—. . . . From you.' "
(298) She sees still farther into the void both when she asks
Jack, " 'Why didn't you want Jasper to come out of the ground?' "
and immediately after the question, when she "stood there
marveling that you could be yourself all those years and not
know you could up and say something like that to an old man
you had loved." (375) She discovers a truer love than her devotion to his legend when she hears his song, and says, " 'Oh
John T.—I never saw you before!' " (402) She has discovered
the Sartrean Other, and her discovery leads her to selfhood; she
adds, " 'Maybe it's because—because I never was me before.' "
(402) Monty, in turn, has at least a glimpse of the real world of
life and death which underlies his realm of hero-worship. He
gains that glimpse through the knowledge, appropriately enough,
of Jo-Lea's pregnancy. He feels "as though, for the first time in
his life, he was himself. It was as though he had never been
Monty Harrick before." (340–341) After his confrontation with
darkness in the form of the mountainside orgy, after holding
Jasper's hand, he will presumably enter the real world.

MacCarland also finds reality, as Warren grapples with the
question of God for the first time since *All the King's Men*.
There, Warren seemed to say that man's goal is an awareness of
and participation in the great web of being, which we may or
may not term God, as we choose. *The Cave* seems consistent
here, in that MacCarland gains selfhood by discovering that God
becomes; that is, He is immanent rather than transcendent and
changes with the organic web of being. Jack, however, in his
philosophical exchange with MacCarland, likens God to Truth
and argues that Truth is no more than the shape of man's needs:
that man will believe what he wants to believe, even if his beliefs
are contradictory. *The Cave*, then, seems still more qualified in
its religious affirmation than *All the King's Men*.

Finally, Nick, too, breaks out of his dream. He begins at the
Harrick cabin where he and Celia come together momentarily in
their common need to give voice to the emptiness within them.
He is about to tell her of his guilt at profiting by her suffering,
when she blurts out the story of Jack's Chattanooga escapade.
Immediately afterwards, trying to comfort her, he has his first

moment of illumination. "He was thinking, or knowing without thinking, that this was the first human face, it seemed, he had ever looked into. Really looked into, just for its humanness." (307) Nick is discovering involvement.

His awareness flowers when his wife refuses to perform an abortion on Jo-Lea, saying, " 'I don't care if I get sent to the poorhouse and die, I am not going to do it to no little girl like her.' " (363) In this indication of caring, Nick can for the first time recognize his wife's humanity. With that recognition, the confection called Giselle Fontaine dies for Nick: "It was as though he had loved somebody and they were dead." Out of that death the human being named Sarah Pumfret is born. Bringing her a glass of water which, as in *Night Rider,* is a sign of human communion, Nick becomes curious about her for the first time. "He wondered what she had looked like when she was a little girl. Fifteen or sixteen. No, eight or nine. He wondered where she had lived. He would have to ask her, some time." (365) Having entered into the web of interpenetration which is true being and which involves man in mankind and in history, Nick can look toward the future: "He tried to think of a day different from what today would be." (364) Thus, Nick joins the company of the saved. Whereas Ikey moves toward the oblivion of false being, they journey toward real life, and the opposing paths give the novel its shape.

An intricate symbolic pattern also helps to shape *The Cave.* Water imagery, so frequent in the first three novels, recurs, again signifying the life of illusion. Jo-Lea listens to the crowd congregated around the cave's entrance and hears "the hum of voices, like distant surf." (316) As Ikey absorbs himself in his elaborate deceit, he momentarily resists his own undertow; "he pulled himself up, like a swimmer." (322) Nick, remembering Giselle Fontaine's night club performance, thinks, "It was as though she had risen there, pure as foam, out of some timelessness like the sea." (176) Jack remembers himself as the little boy who disobeyed his mother and went swimming, while Celia remembers him on the back of the pickup truck "riding the sway like a sailor on a tossing deck." (160)

Light-dark imagery, central to *Band of Angels,* also recurs.

Once again darkness, like water, symbolizes false being, and the two images frequently reinforce each other. Thus, Ikey's undertow is "the dark, coiling depth of the waves" (322), and, as he leaves home, conscious that MacCarland is not watching him go down the stairs, he "felt the fear of being thrown absolutely upon his own frail resources, alone, dropped into a sea, at night." (359) Nick's moment of awareness comes with the dawn; Jack's moment of terror occurs at night and is "like waking up in the dark and not knowing who you are." (144) Insects and moths batter the screens of the Harrick cabin, irritating Jack in their struggle for illumination.[3] As Ikey flees Johntown, he barrels through a red light with the comment, " 'Fuck the light.' " (367) Earlier, worn out with his triumphant deceptions, Ikey floats "like a feather in the dark at the hollow center of the world." (333)

This metaphor indicates the connection between darkness and cave; the actual cave imagery draws together the imagery of water and darkness, and completes the symbolic pattern. The memory which terrifies Ikey involves "the black pit with the narrow shelf along the pit; and . . . the sound of water from the deep blackness." (184) The image of the dark cave appears in Warren's fiction as early as *Night Rider*, when Mr. Munn's doubts verge horribly into self-doubts as he contemplates the cavernous dark of the world with its snowfall. The cave-darkness-water cluster has also appeared before, so that Jack Burden's castigation of Tiny Duffy ("a mean worry on your mind and a great blackness like water rising in a cellar inside you") comes to mind when McCarland Sumpter is described as feeling "as though a level of black water rose from the floor to overwhelm him, as though he himself were only an agony of emptiness, into which the blackness flowed." (83)

But whereas Warren has previously made symbolic use of the cave, here, as title and epigraph indicate, it has become the controlling metaphor of unreality. This "hollow center of the world" is the cave of Plato's parable, which depicts men who

---

3. The moth symbolism is noted in Richard Davison, "Robert Penn Warren's 'Dialectical Configuration' and *The Cave*," p. 351.

live their lives in a cave and therefore lack any true conception of reality; it is the void of limitation and false being into which men fall away. Thus Jack, catching a glimpse of his emptiness, thinks, "It looked like there was a big black hole right in the middle of him where a man's thinking and feeling and living ought to be, and he was going to fall into the hole and fall forever into the black nothing." (139) When Ikey remembers his initial exploration of the cave with Jasper, he recalls not only the dark pit and the sound of water, but also "what the flashlight beam had showed then, the great cathedral pillars rising to the arches of ceiling, the dome beyond studded, in the light, with ghostly gypsum flowers." (184) The cathedral in the cave is the false being with which men try to fill their voids, but succeed only in structuring them; like Milton's Pandaemonium,[4] it is built in hell, a temple to fragmentation and falsehood.

This analysis of the cave makes possible a reconsideration of Jasper and of his relationship to the cave. Leonard Casper finds something positive in that relationship, and wonders whether Jasper does not enter the cave because he has discovered "some superior stage in the act of transcendence . . . which liberates his spirit for enjoyment of the immutable timeless-as-eternity."[5] In support of this possibility, Casper points to Monty's description of Jasper "with the whole earth tucked in around him."[6] In the passage which Casper quotes, Monty, enviously picturing Jasper, thinks,

He would toss 'em what they craved and just laugh his easygoing way and off to the woods again, or drift down the river in his skiff, miles and miles, nobody knew where, flat on his back in the skiff, his hat over his face against the sunlight, dreaming in the darkness of his head, drifting on . . . into nighttime, all night long, and alone, or go wandering off, not merely to deep woods or down river, but crawl down in the ground, in the caves, deeper and deeper, lying in the ground with his dreaming, as though he had cave-crawled into the

---

4. John Milton, *Paradise Lost*, Book I, ll. 700–757.

5. Leonard Casper, "Journey to the Interior: *The Cave*," *Modern Fiction Studies* (Spring 1960), reprinted in *Robert Penn Warren: A Collection of Critical Essays*, ed. John L. Longley Jr., p. 151.

6. Casper, "Journey to the Interior," p. 151.

earth like it was some sort of joyous dark-dreaming he was crawling into, to lie snug and complete with the whole earth tucked in around him. (19)

The imagery of the passage, with its emphasis on darkness, dreaming, cave and river, indicates an unreality very different from the vitality and freedom which Monty infers in his concluding interpretation. Monty, as victim of his hero-worship, is hardly a reliable narrator, particularly when interpreting his hero's actions.

Does Monty's unreality color his observations themselves? His imagery, as a simple recollection of facts perceived, would seem reliable, as other accounts of Jasper confirm. Jo-Lea sees in her mind's eye "the image of Jasper Harrick, alone on a gray boulder above tumbled water, wearing a red shirt, playing his box, his head thrown back, singing to the solitude." (317) Here Jasper appears bound to Jack, not only through the guitar but through his red shirt, which imitates Jack's red mackinaw just as Monty's boots imitate Jasper's. Jo-Lea sees Jasper's image because, as Jack finally senses, Jasper has no reality; Jack says to Jo-Lea, " 'You just got Jasper and Monty sort of mixed, didn't you? Like a dream gets sort of mixed with daylight.' " (391) Jo-Lea sees Jasper on the river, where he tries to escape his dilemma just as he later will in the cave. Celia recognizes this attempt at escape, blaming Jack. Jasper admits to it when he tells Celia, " 'A lot of things don't matter down there,' " and says, describing the climate of the cave, " 'It is not summer and it is not winter. There aren't any seasons to worry about." (240) These comments within the context of *The Cave* and of Warren's earlier novels, have unmistakable meaning. As fugitive from reality seeking out the cave, Jasper gives himself to the void, which claims him.

The cave in its broadest reaches, then, is the existential void; in its narrowest sense, the cave is sexual, as the orgy in progress around the cave suggests. Charles Bohner notes womb-tomb connotations,[7] which are, indeed, quite explicit. Celia, for example, thinks, "She had been about four months pregnant with

7. Charles Bohner, *Robert Penn Warren*, p. 150.

Jasper then and now, so many years later, with Jasper stuck in a hole in the ground." (295) And the woman on the mountain-side offers herself to Monty with the words, " 'it's a cold hole he's in—but you, sweetheart—' " (347) The rampant sexuality of the novel is a deadly thing, a grotesque parody of life and communion. At its best, it is Rachel "arming" herself for Ikey; at its worst it is Jack regretting his betrayal of legend on the mountain with Celia and wondering what would have happened if "he had turned and seized her, not falling on his knees, and ripped her, and ripped out of her what he wanted, and flung her aside on the grass." (151) Or again, it is the woman on the mountain drawing Monty's hand to her as she asks, " 'What do you think of that muff, Buster?' " (346) The laying-on of hands which signifies communion (Jack's song, Monty-Jasper, etc.) [8] is directly antithetical to the inhumanity of this sexual contact, which characterizes every sexual relationship in the novel.

The cave-womb is the place of fallenness, but it can also prove fruitful.[9] The apparent ambiguity inherent in the cave derives from the nature of the existential void itself; the sticking point for Casper has perhaps been the simple paradox that the negative can prove positive. The key is awareness. As the conversion of Jack Harrick (to choose one character) indicates, the acknowledgment of the void leads to a sense of involvement and responsibility, and the whole of selfhood. Jasper, unable to bear involvement and assume responsibility for himself, caught in the unreality of Jack's legends, is caught in the cave. Once Jasper lies there, the cave offers the possibility of involvement, and so functions as a symbolic counterpart to the redemptive process. Ikey, unable to bear the acknowledgment of the void which makes

8. Leonard Casper first commented on the significance of touch as communion in his "Journey to the Interior," p. 155. For a detailed discussion, see the excellent article by James H. Justus, "The Use of Gesture in Warren's *The Cave*."

9. Charles Bohner makes this point concerning Ikey: mistakenly, I think. He points to Ikey's sense, while in the cave, of a "self, a free, immortal self, ready for song." Bohner, *Warren*, p. 151. That "free, immortal self" is clearly a false self.

involvement possible, lacks the courage to go into the cave to
Jasper. Jebb Holloway, whose surname indicates his relationship
to the void, is still more afraid of the cave than Ikey. Monty
and MacCarland, on the other hand, have both confronted
nothingness: Monty in the mountainside orgy, MacCarland in
recognizing his self-deceptions. Both have also accepted involvement: Monty in his prospective fatherhood, MacCarland in
his love for his son. And so MacCarland and Monty are both
able to go into the cave to Jasper, and come out into the real
world.

A brilliant and related symbol underscores the paradox of the
negative proving positive. Jack's guitar is a "box" throughout; as
a general analogue, through its hollowness, of the cave,[10] and as
a very specific analogue, through its most vulgar connotations, of
the cave-womb, it suggests on the one hand the coffin-void, the
escapist's womb, and on the other hand, the fruitful womb.
Initially it is Young Jack's unreality, the symbol of his sensual
sovereignty, with its arrogant inscription, "His Box." When
Jack reforms, he puts it aside; Jasper, the crown prince, takes it
up. When Jasper flees to the cave, he leaves it behind, together
with the boots which have similar symbolic value. (Thus Monty
wears duplicates.) Finally, in the darkened room where Jack
discovers both his emptiness and the web, he picks up the guitar;
out of its hollowness emanates harmony, as the dark becomes
luminous.

By quoting *The Republic* for his epigraph, Warren turns
Plato against himself. Although *The Cave* is Platonic in defining
sexuality as a dream, Warren, unlike Plato, refuses to locate
reality in the ideal. Warren, in his monistic system, allows no
such idealism. Ikey in his dream of academic triumph, Mac-
Carland in his dream of God, are both drawn toward the cave.
Even Truth and God are finally discredited as Absolutes, and,
redefined as the creations of need, are drawn into the web of
being. Any flight from that web is directed toward irresponsibility
and into the cave, the womb of unreality which promises protection from the asperities of real existence. Thus Jasper can flee

10. Casper, "Journey to the Interior," p. 155.

Jack's legend and yet die in the cave; the externalized, public existence of Jack clanging his anvil for the town and the internalized, isolate existence of Jasper playing his guitar for the river are one in their unreality. Jasper is like Sartre's Jonah in the story of that name, who, after living first the public and then the private life, dies with one word written on a piece of paper: that word is either "solidaire" or "solitaire." No one can determine which because the two are indistinguishable as forms of false being.

Warren's previous novels, in portraying the dualism of that unreality, suggest that the world is a swamp and the idea a dream. What *The Cave* contributes to the development of Warren's canon is a clearer understanding that the passion of lust does not differ significantly from the passion of asceticism, or, to put the matter differently, that the world, too, has its dream. As Warren has said elsewhere, not some, but all men seek to justify.[11] Even the man of the quagmire has a dream with which he justifies himself in trying to fill the void. And finally, *The Cave* makes clear that the dream of the world, however physical, resembles the dream of the ideal in that each is an abstraction, for each involves the attempt to view in isolation what can only be seen in context.

11. Robert Penn Warren, " 'The Great Mirage: Conrad and *Nostromo*," in *Selected Essays*, pp. 43–44.

CHAPTER VII

Wilderness

ADAM ROSENZWEIG, the protagonist of *Wilderness*, resembles Manty Starr in that he searches for freedom and, lacking will, floats on the tide of events. The freedom which Adam seeks, however, unlike Manty's, is the pure Platonic ideal, so that he makes one with the idealistic brotherhood of Tobias Sears and Jeremiah Beaumont. Like them, he embarks on a spiritual pilgrimage which ends in the saving awareness that such abstraction denies the very fabric of life.

Adam's journey begins in Bavaria, where he inherits his father Leopold's idealism. Years before, Leopold had written, "If I could only be worthy of that mountain I love, / If I could only be worthy of sun-glitter on snow, / If man could only be worthy of what he loves." (5) Leopold's ideal is human potentiality and political freedom; "He had told his son that there was no nobler fate for a man than to live and die for human liberty." (7) On his deathbed, however, to Adam's dismay, Leopold renounces the ideal which has shaped his life. In doing so he unwittingly leaves the torch for Adam to take up; "And Adam knew that, in that very moment, in that shadowy room, when his father's self had died, his own self had been born." (9)

Adam's new self is born in a "shadowy room" because the adopted ideal, however noble it might be, is, like all the ideals which Warren depicts, shadowy and unreal. Warren's remarks on the old Garibaldino of *Nostromo* apply both to Adam and to

Leopold: "He believes in the human bond, in a brotherhood of liberty, and has risked his life in the hope of bringing the day of liberty nearer to man; but . . . his idealism is tainted with abstraction."[1] Thus, viewing his Bavarian surroundings in their ugliness, Adam thinks how his father "had lifted his eyes above those things to the glittering whiteness of the mountain, and had yearned . . . to be worthy of the mountain he loved." (6) In *Wilderness,* Warren tells of a journey leading, not up from the fallen world to the Celestial City, but down from the heavenly mountain and into a world redeemed.

A central symbol in the novel is Adam's congenitally crippled foot, which represents the human flaw, man's limitation. Adam gives himself over to unreality by disowning that limitation, by contriving a corrective boot "that very instant when, in the darkening room, six months before, his father had repudiated his own life." (17) The boot represents the false being of Adam's inherited abstraction, and, as such, bears the marks of artifice, of reality betrayed; it is "the bright, strange, clever boot" of "cunning design" and "concealed height." (16)

Thus shod, Adam is ready to begin his pilgrimage, which proves to consist of a series of collisions between the ideal he cherishes and the world he confronts. His uncle in Bavaria laughs at his idea of freedom. On the ship bound for New York, his foot betrays him, as it conspicuously buckles. His fellow recruits also betray him. When Duncan angrily demands to know why he, a cripple, has come, Adam listens to an unreal inner voice answer, " 'I came . . . because I wanted to fight for freedom .' " (23) And once again, Adam's affirmation of his ideal is greeted by the laughter of the world, this time in a great chorus led by a character with the appropriate name of Pig-Eye.

At this early stage, however, Adam is able to resist disillusionment by gilding his experience. After Duncan has turned him over to the sailors to earn his trip back home, he scrubs decks and chips rust from chairs "laxly dragging his boot behind him, ac-

1. Robert Penn Warren, " 'The Great Mirage': Conrad and *Nostromo,*" in *Selected Essays,* p. 36.

cepting again, as it were, a sense of his crippledness." (27) Adam
rescues himself from this potentially saving sense of limitation
by thinking that the derisive cry "Für die Freiheit!" had not
ended in derision. "Perhaps in repeating that cry over and over,
the men who had begun it in derision found it springing from
their own deepest need." (28) At this point, Adam finds further
solace in remembering Old Jacob, the Bavarian shoemaker who
made the corrective boot. Apprenticed as a boy, Jacob had run
away because he could not bear the smell of manure-cured
leather. Caught and returned, he has managed to adapt to the
world, and he chews on a piece of leather, swallowing the saliva,
to show Adam that " 'I have learned to live.' " (31) But despite
his adjustment to the world, Jacob refuses to accept payment for
the boot, saying that he needs more than the knowledge of
having learned to live. " 'I must have the knowledge that my
boot has walked on the earth in America. . . . The boot is
mine—I have paid for it by learning how to live.' " (32) Jacob's
story has meanings which run counter to Adam's idealism:
manure-cured leather is the stuff of the idealistic boot, a boot
which is to be earned through experience. Adam, however, feeds
his devotion to the idea by seeing in the story only Jacob's
yearning for some ideal.

Adam similarly twists his experience with the seaman who
offers him a plan of escape from the ship, then claims to have
helped only as an exercise in ingenuity. There seems little of the
idealist in the sailor, who speaks contemptuously of the immi-
grants as cannon fodder and of Adam as a "ruddy fool" headed
for a fall. But Adam, determined that the sailor has acted out of
sympathy for freedom, says to him, " 'You're not telling the
truth.' " (38) In each case, Adam manipulates his experience to
nourish his idealism.

In America, however, world and idea as Adam conceives them
break apart. He first meets with a hanged and mutilated Negro,
and then with a rampant mob in the process of murdering more
Negroes. Upon learning that the murderers are native New
Yorkers and not invading Rebels, Adam is forced to conclude
that the land of liberty does not share in his worship of liberty
and that even in America he is alone in his devotion to idea.

A fate like Jasper Harrick's nearly brings Adam's American tour to an abrupt conclusion, as he barely escapes drowning in a dark cellar, the victim of his illusions.

Adam emerges from this brush with the void determined to maintain his idea in the face of adversity. As he journeys to Virginia as sutler, the world he travels seems devoid of idea, and even his companions mock his idealism. Adam explains to Mose why Leopold had named him 'Adam': " 'My father gave me that name because he loved mankind and wanted men to be fully man. He fought and suffered for that. He gave me that name that I might try to be a man in the knowledge that men are by brothers." (91–92) He asks that Mose call him 'Adam' to help him be worthy of the name, but Mose chooses instead to call him 'Slew.' Once again, the world refuses to countenance Adam's idea.

Several of the people encountered on his journey reinforce Adam's impression of a world in darkness. Simms Purdue, Union hero, desecrates the ideal for which he has fought by having camp Negroes dunk their heads in flour to root for dollars with their mouths. Mordecai Sulgrave, as his surname suggests, is a grave robber, and his actions mock the idea of heroic sacrifice which he ironically exalts. And Mollie the Mutton, camp follower, seems to mock every ideal with her sexual largesse.

Even a meeting with Hans Meyerhof, like Leopold a veteran of Rastatt, provides only a moment of joy. For that moment Adam sees in the dying Hans "a father who had handled a musket at Rastatt but who, in dying—dying with a rifle ball in him taken in another war and another place—would not repudiate the old truth." (120) But Hans has not known Leopold, and in his feeble words Adam recognizes "a voice weak, dry, distant, a voice not out of Time, but in Time, marked by Time. . . . The moment of bliss was gone. He had to live in Time. He had only what he had to live by, and with." (121) The dream withers in its exposure to the world: for Adam, "the self that had once existed and had had that dream no longer existed. Only the dry, pale shell, like that discarded by a locust, existed now." (99)

Adam sustains this hollow, false self with the thought of two acts, each apparently performed out of selfless devotion to an ideal. Jed Hawksworth, Adam's boss, has, as a young man, stood up in court to defend a Negro against the false charges of father and friends, and Mose has saved Adam from drowning in the New York cellar. Both acts are abruptly discredited as examples of selflessness. Jed explains to Adam that he stood up in court not out of any sense of brotherhood of justice, but because of outraged pride at his father's flagrant toadying. " 'I hated them for being ashamed for my pa. . . . And I hated my pa for making me ashamed of him.' " (160) Mose similarly frustrates Adam's expectation. Adam has assumed that Mose saved him from drowning through some sense of brotherhood and human worth. When Mose is quite literally exposed as a deserter, drawers stripped off to bare the brand of 'W' for 'worthless,' Adam views the desertion as a betrayal of brotherhood and asks why Mose, apparently lacking any such ideal, had acted to save him. Mose explains, " 'If'n you tried to climb up— if'n you got clawen and couldn't make it—and maken a racket— then all them folks might of tried to climb up thar. . . . An' that shelf, hit warn't room fer but two.' " (221) Each explanation acknowledges only the selfish motive and leaves Adam feeling cheated; he asks Mose, " 'Was that it? Was that all?' " (221) And he wonders, "Was no man, in his simple humanity, more to any other man than a stir or voice, a sloshing in the dark?" (224)

Adam, however, in his abstraction, has no more regard for the individual "in his simple humanity" than does anyone he encounters. The keynote of his cold detachment sounds early in the novel, when his uncle in Bavaria, trying to dissuade him from going to America to fight, says, " 'Know that when even the righteous man righteously persecutes even the wicked, God yet weeps for the persecuted.' " Adam, with a flicker of "cold joy," answers, " 'I do not believe that God weeps . . . when the wicked are persecuted to bring Justice. Nor do I weep for them.' " (16) Nor does he weep for the innocent, persecuted in the name of injustice, if he can avoid weeping. He marvels himself at the fact that his blood-sympathy for the hanged man had waned on the instant of recognizing his blackness—a blackness which is as symbolic as Manty Starr's.

Adam lacks a vision of humanity, and so looks on men with an unseeing eye. He is like Jed Hawksworth, who, when addressed, might "fix upon the speaker a blankness of unrecognition. . . . The speaker's very existence would be called into question." (95) Thus, while Hans Meyerhof pleads for understanding, Adam sees, not Hans, but Leopold. When Blaustein tries to adopt him as son to succeed the dead Stephen, Adam once again sees, not the speaker, but his own father, "magically rising beyond pain and distemper of spirit to welcome his son into his triumph." (77–78) Adam, that is, looks at the world but sees only the idea, pure and indomitable. Blaustein points to Adam's foot and says, " 'It is a sign,' " meaning that it will keep Adam from fighting and force him to remain as Blaustein's son. Adam, however, sees, not the foot, but the boot; rapt in his own dream, he says, " 'It is my boot.' " (78) He feels Balustein's need only as a trap: "a thousand filmy strands being cast over him, binding him, netting him down." (78) He rejects that need, saying, " 'I want something from you . . . surprised at the distant harshness of his voice." (79)

Even in his progressive disillusionment, Adam will not, and in fact, cannot allow himself any commitment to another person. He will not, because, moral absolutist that he is, he views the world as impurity and temptation; he cannot, because his lingering devotion to idea continues to isolate him from the real world. His abortive relationship with Maran Meyerhof is an example, but the full measure of his removal from mankind is his relationship with Mose, whom Adam, as idealist, prizes more in theory than in person. Events lead Adam to undertake teaching Mose his letters. When Mose presents his misshapen efforts, Adam forces a compliment "and tried to put heartiness into the tone, to keep from betraying what, suddenly and inexplicably, he felt—the hopelessness, the aimlessness, and in his very guts, the revulsion. If only those eyes had not worn that naked appeal." (181) The misshapen letters reflect Adam's own deformity and suggest his involvement in man's limitation, an involvement which the pleading eyes implore. But the suggestion and the plea appall Adam, for they threaten to pull him down from his mountain.

Adam fails more significantly to respond to Mose's human

appeal when Mose, exposed as deserter, reaches out in his humiliation for understanding. Mose insists that he would rather have been fatally wounded in battle than have been forced to serve in the army as a mere beast of burden. He pleads, " 'You gotta believe me, Slew. I'd ruther be layen thar bleeden. Layen thar and the blood comen out—God durn it, Slew, I swear—I swear—' " (222) But, to Adam, Mose has lost his symbolic significance through his desertion and his admission of self-interest in saving Adam; and for Adam in his cold abstraction, the man without such significance as custodian of the ideal has no significance at all. He rejects the appeal.

> "Shut up!" Adam cried into the darkness.
> "Shut up, and get to bed, you—you—" His breath would not come. Then, with a sweet rush, his breath came, and a joy filled his being, as though in the darkness nobody were there, as though he himself were about to fill all the dark and be, for the first time, totally himself.
> "You—yes, you—" he cried, "you—you black son-of-a-bitch." (222–223)

Once again Adam looks without seeing, "as though . . . nobody were there"; he looks at human need and sees only the deserter, the false savior, the betrayer of the idea. In turning away from Mose, Adam temporarily joins the brotherhood of Ikey Sumpter, who also became "totally himself" in the darkness of his alienation from mankind. He gives himself over to the void, "as though he himself were about to fill all the dark."

Mose's response is to murder Jed; when Adam discovers the corpse, a great uncaring universe seems to absorb him. He thinks, "They will accuse me. They will hold me. Who will care what will happen to me. Innocent or guilty, who will care? . . . Who cares about anything?" (230) With this new vision of the world, Adam finds a new freedom, the freedom of indifference. Deciding to leave the retreating sutlers and beat on alone into Virginia, he pulls off the road and feels confirmed in his course by the indifference of the passing caravan, "those whose stare of uninterest had bleached him into nothingness." (236) Three men show some interest, and they too offer confirmation. One spits, the second tries to kill Adam over a trivial matter, and the third intervenes on Adam's behalf only to offer Adam financial inducement to leave Jed's employ for his, apparently assuming that cash forms the only bond between men. The sutlers having departed, Adam stands liberated from the world: "Suddenly, all the past was nothing, and joy flooded his heart. He was free, at last, to go." (245)

This freedom is, of course, potentially disastrous, for it verges on complete dissociation from the real world and its redeeming human bond. Adam now introduces himself by saying, " 'I am a foreigner. I come from Bavaria. That is in Germany. I am a Jew. I do not care which side is which. I want to sell things.' " (250–251) At this point, Adam is ready for his meeting with Monmorancy Pugh, whose corruption is evident in both of his names. His wife tells Adam how, determined not to participate in the war and take human life, he killed the conscripter; then, in flight, he found the peace of the quagmire in a new picture of the world. Pugh imagines that God has placed man in this world hanging by his hands from a limb over an abyss, and, having left man thus, God then proceeds to tickle his feet to make him scratch. Pugh contends that he has scratched once and intends to keep right on scratching. In his brutish falling away, he joins the company of men with unseeing eye; Mrs. Pugh tells Adam, " 'He went past me lak I warn't thar.' " (258) So completely does Monmorancy Pugh question the reality of others that the question has become a denial, and he murders pickets for their belongings. His is the ultimate dissociation.

But while Adam has undergone gradual disillusionment and earned his place with the Pughs by slowly withdrawing from the community of men into indifference, he has also had, from the beginning of his quest, an intimation of the real world and its dark ties. Contemplating the Negro hanged by the mob, "With a gush of shame, even of desperation, he thought that as soon as he recognized the man as black, the deepest, instinctive blood-sympathy had begun to ebb. *Can I be that vile?* he demanded of himself? *Oh, can I be?*" (45) Here Adam senses his participation in what Tobias Sears has called "the falling nature of the world," the world's falling away from true being. Although Adam can sense that participation, he cannot accept it, and thus his sense of the communion which that participation entails cannot realize itself. Thinking with hatred of Simms Purdue, he hears an inner voice saying, *"I must not hate him, I must not hate him or I shall die."* (165) The thought brings joy, as he perceives the necessary communion which would result from Simms Purdue's confiding of a boyhood incident. But the joy is only momentary, for Adam does not yet know how to reconcile his hatred with the need for communion of his own accord, without the overture from Simms Purdue.

Gradually Adam learns that he has mistaken the object of his hatred. He pictures Mose in flight, "ready to start up with guilty fear at any sound, leaning by a single candle flame while his big hand gripped a pencil and copied a letter from a card. Seeing that image, he felt an unmanning constriction in his chest. Something too complicated, too terrible for him to give a name to was in him, was in the world." (231–232) With this discovery that "something terrible" is shared, Adam is ready for his next burst of awareness. As the caravan of unconcerned sutlers passes by, he thinks, *"They accuse me of being like them. But I'm not, I'm not,* he protested. Then: *But they hate me because I am.* Then: *I hate them because I am."* (237) Adam realizes that his hatred has its source in self-hatred, but he cannot yet come to terms with the realization. "At that, the rage and shame roiled up in him" (237), and he proceeds to desert the caravan.

What Adam must learn is that (as Aaron Blaustein has said) "everything is a part of everything else": that the world and the idea, which he views as separate, are inextricably intertwined in the web of being, so that motives, for example, are neither as pure as he demands nor as corrupt as he suspects. The scene in which Simms Purdue dunks Negroes in flour will serve to illustrate. Adam attempts to intervene; by this point in the novel it seems clear that he acts as much through abstract need as out of kindness. Mose restrains Adam, explaining that he merely wishes to keep his teacher intact; since the army provides teachers, the explanation seems less than candid. The episode with the Pughs involves a similar ambivalence, evident in the name "Monmorancy Pugh." Pugh intends from the start to kill Adam;

but Adam is twice saved, once by Monmorancy himself, with the explanation, " 'A man gits tahrd,' " and once by Mrs. Pugh, who gives Adam the unloaded pistol. The entire episode evinces the stench of nothingness apparent in their surname together with the humanity which saves Adam.

But although he responds to Mrs. Pugh's story by reaching out and touching her, an action whose significance *The Cave* makes abundantly clear, he seems largely oblivious of whatever meaning the episode might convey. Momentarily this is not so. Thinking of Mollie the Mutton as he is about to fall asleep in the cabin, he wonders what had happened to her, and envisions himself comforting her. "A strange excitement took him. He felt himself trembling on the verge of a revelation. It was a revelation not, he suddenly decided, about Mollie the Mutton. Except insofar as Mollie was a part of the world. For it was a revelation about the world. The whole world. It was not about flight from the world, but about the nature of the world. He was about to put the truth into words. Then, all at once, he was asleep." (253) But even as revelation escapes him here, he remains controlled by images rather than realities. A few minutes before his thoughts of Mollie, watching Mrs. Pugh, he no longer sees the worn face or broken tooth, and thinks, "What did anything matter in the great emptiness of the world when now he saw the calmness and purity of the silhouette against the rosy light?" (252) Adam's own being remains divided even this late in the novel, with Adam still seeking the purity of the silhouette rather than the reality of worn flesh and still unaware of the web. His stay with the Pughs ends in a symbolic journey of mythic proportions across the river and into the wilderness, with Pugh as guide. The endpoint is the void: the death which Pugh has planned and the wilderness itself are analogues.

Alone in that void, Adam begins the final leg of his journey to selfhood. Feeling "disembodied and pure," he is reminded of himself as a boy, recovering from a long fever, "feeling himself adrift in air, light as a feather, pure." (285) He remembers, too, his mother coming in to him, and thinks, *That was the last time she ever loved me.* She had, he could think now with distant sadness, come to hate him because he had not forgiven her for not forgiving his father. 'Your father,' she had once said, 'he thought more of something else than of me. Or of you.' And the boy, caught up in rage and rapture, had cried: 'And so do I! And so do I!' " (286) Now Adam can perceive the coldness of that rapture. "Sitting here now, in broad daylight, he heard, with a wrench of the heart, the very words the boy had cried, and saw, again, the woman's stricken face. In the vividness of that vision, here in the woods of this far country, he was about to rise, to cry out, no, no, it was not that he didn't love her, it was something different, something he had to explain to her, if she would only listen, if she would only—" (286) As his growing compassion begins to shape his thoughts, Adam glimpses the void in the form of his destructive abstraction, his own falling away, and is "about to rise." He sees his isolation in a new light, thinking "that he, he himself, was the cold center of stillness in the storm which was the world." (290) In his journey home to his mother, Adam begins to repair his broken link with the real world.

Now when the most dramatic clash between reality and abstraction occurs, Adam is ready for understanding. Confederate soldiers materialize out of the woods and, in the process of looting the wagon, relieve Adam of his boots, including of course, the corrective boot which is no longer his, now that he recognizes the destructiveness of his abstraction. In the scuffle which ensues when Union soldiers appear, Adam, outraged at the unevenness of the contest, grabs a rifle and in the name of freedom and justice kills a Confederate. Alone with the corpse, he muses on his unexpected act and at first exults over having redeemed his ideal. "Nothing had been able to stop him, he thought. He felt a surge of pride in that, a manliness." (300) Then his attitude changes. "He looked down again at his bare feet. He thought how white, friendless, and unfended they looked in the middle of the glade, with the woods darkening. All at once he felt sorry for them—not for himself, but for them as though they were stupid, ugly, unlovable children, lost, not knowing." (300) Suddenly, in the void, Adam sees the human limitation ("stupid, ugly, unlovable") and false being ("children, lost, not knowing") which his "Christian" name proclaims, the false being which is the ignorance of innocence.

Adam, then, looks at his crippled foot and sees not only his own defect but the shared darkness; this consideration leads in turn to a sense of responsibility for himself and others. He realizes that his "hardness of heart" has killed Aaron Blaustein and Jed Hawksworth, while making a murderer of Mose Crawford alias Talbutt. Wondering why Mose did not kill him rather than Jed, Adam concludes that *"you cannot strike down what you have lifted up.* So Jed, he decided, had had to die in his place. And then, with that thought, he wondered if every man is, in the end, a sacrifice for every other man. He did not know. He could not read the depth of the thought." (302) Here Adam sees the great web of interrelationship.

But the vision is too staggering to bear, and, in a typical example of the ebb and flow of Adam's false being, he slips back into his easy absolutism. Aaron Blaustein, Jedeen Hawksworth, Mose Crawford, and his father, he thinks, have all betrayed the idea of man's nobility, and if that nobility is so vulnerable, then the defect alone can be man's strength, for it is the only constant, the only given. "He looked down at the twisted whiteness of his poor foot. . . . *My father,* he thought, *that is what he gave me.* He felt that he was on the verge of a great truth. He felt that everything he had ever known was false. *Ah,* he thought, that is the greatest betrayal." (303) Like the sons in *Band of Angels,* Adam blames the father for his limitation, and even more, for the abstractions which made him condemn that limitation. With his ideal discredited, a false legacy, Adam decides to appropriate the dead man's boots as replacements for those taken from him, for "that was the way the world was." (303)

Filled with the thought of the world's animality, he feels liberated from all restraints.[2] His god is dead, and everything is possible. "He was dizzy with a sudden access of power. He had

2. I find myself in agreement with Cleanth Brooks. *The Hidden God,* p 124.

never felt anything like this. Deep in his being he was aware, fleetingly, of an image, a rich room glittering with crystal and silver, yellow hair falling unbound, candlelight winking redly through wine, a white breast lifted to his hand." (304) Adam's newfound vision of an amoral, anarchic freedom, like the vision of Monmorancy Pugh and the legend of Jack Harrick, threatens as much of an abstraction from the fabric of selfhood as that caused earlier by his allegiance to pure idea. Once again he yields to illusion, feeling free of the world and innocent. "He felt suddenly pure, and young. All the past was suddenly nothing." (304)

But Adam is drawn back toward reality. He notices, in the debris of the wagon, his uncle's satchel; once again the past is something. He remembers how Blaustein's maid had worked to restore his prayer book from its cellar soaking and regrets that he did not even look inside it. "He wished he had opened the book before her eyes and praised her. Why hadn't he done it? It would have been so easy." (305) This sense of caring is directly antithetical to the sense of power which he has just previously experienced. Removing the boot he has just put on, placing it beside the corpse, he looks at the dead man's face and wonders what his own face will be like in death; once again he accepts his limitation and sees himself within the context of humanity. He realizes that the burning wilderness of his isolation is an inferno and has his final insight in a moment of vision; for the first time, Adam sees. He sees men wounded, crippled, and lost: mankind trying to see, crying out soundlessly in the darkness, reaching out for the touch of communion.

Adam's response to his vision of community is a prayer for God's mercy and man's understanding. Earlier, Adam has been contemptuous of both, so that the prayer indicates a new humility in the face of human imperfection and need. The prayer is that spoken at the burial of his father in Bavaria, so that, with Adam's acceptance of his place in the human community, past and present coalesce. As he speaks the words of the prayer, "that place and this place, and that time and this time, flowed together." (308) Once again, he begins to don the dead man's boots. Reborn, he will no longer try to deny man's defect as he has previously done with his cunning boot and his idea of man's nobility. But neither will he exult in darkness and the license it implies. He has discovered the significance of Blaustein's key statements: "The hardest thing to remember is that other men are men" (67), and "Everything is part of everything else." (74) He takes the boots humbly, this time, with a sense of the men who had previously worn them and "of what they, as men and in their error, had endured." (310) Reunited with humanity, he does not renounce his former quest, but reaffirms it, adding a crucial modification: "Yes, he thought, staring at the rifle, he would do it all again. . . . *But oh, with a different heart!*" (310) In the light of awareness, the spirit of the quest changes from alienation to involvement: a new will is born.

In some respects, *Wilderness* differs markedly from Warren's earlier novels. It has no digression, no subplot, none of Warren's usual variety of major and minor characters. Warren has said that, in *Wilderness*, he tried "to write the particular story,"[3] which seems to involve a more detailed examination of the struggle for selfhood. Each of the earlier novels after *Night Rider* tends to be schematic, with one or more conversions coming somewhat abruptly at the end. In *Wilderness*, Warren seems determined to show that the process of conversion is intermittent, riddled with backslidings, and unending.

But, if *Wilderness* resists schematization, it nonetheless has a thematic shape which marks no change in Warren's metaphysic. According to the epigraph from Pascal, man is a king dispossessed of his heavenly—or Edenic—kingdom. By acknowledging the wretchedness of his dispossession, by assuming responsibility for his finitude, he becomes great, regaining at least a part of the lost kingdom. He wins his way to a New Jerusalem, thereby transforming his dispossession into something of a fortunate fall. His burden, however, is not simply his finitude, but all human finitude, and the arguments in the epigraph from

3. Correspondence between Casper and Robert Penn Warren as quoted in Casper, "Trial by Wilderness: Warren's Exemplum," *Wisconsin Studies in Contemporary Literature*, 3 (Fall 1962), reprinted in *Robert Penn Warren: A Collection of Critical Essays*, ed. John L. Longley Jr., p. 159.

Henry V are therefore specious in their insistence on irresponsibility. *All* the king's men are spotted and in their spottedness are the responsibility of the king as Pascal defines him: the man who embraces "la grandeur de l'homme" by accepting that responsibility.

CHAPTER VIII

Flood

IN *AT HEAVEN'S GATE,* Jerry Calhoun, returning by air-plane to his home valley, has a momentary vision in which "the late light, layered, striated, and rippling, was like the substance of a crystalline sea which had risen again, on the instant, to drown out that valley."[1] In *Flood,* the imagined inundation oc-curs, and, for the first time, Warren's water imagery lies at the very center of his novel.

As in the earlier novels, water in *Flood* is the destructive ele-ment of unreality. Apostle of the rising tide is Digby, who is one of the engineers building the dam which will flood out Fiddlers-burg, and who sounds like Bogan Murdock as he expounds on the benefits of the dam.

The dam was going to be great, the young engineer said. Going to be near a hundred square miles under water, going to back up the water for twenty-five miles, he had said, gesturing south, up-river. Most of the land not much but swamp or second growth. And what good land there was—hell, they didn't know how to farm it anyway. But with power and cheap transportation it would all be different. A real skyline on the river, plant after plant. Getting shoes on the swamp rats, too, teaching 'em to read and write and punch a time clock, and pull a switch. It was going to be a big industrial complex, he said. He liked the phrase, industrial complex. (113)

1. Robert Penn Warren, *At Heaven's Gate* p. 10.

The narrator's contempt for Digby is quite apparent in this passage. For Digby, progress is power, cheap transportation, and an industrial skyline; progress is the conversion of swamp rats into robots, who will punch time clocks and pull switches. Within Warren's theoretical framework, such progress is radically unreal, a perversion of the natural; the water is unreal as it is perverted by the dam.[2]

Mechanization, then, is symptomatic of false being; Digby applauds industrialization, and Brad, the novel's protagonist (whose name is itself indicative), appears on the scene driving a Jaguar, emblem of the perversion of nature. As Brad approaches Fiddlersburg, he observes nature washed away by unreality. Sycamore, willow tangle, bluegrass and dogwood have given way to a landscape of artifice: Happy Dell and the Seven Dwarfs Motel. "The creek was there, but it flowed decorously between two banks where stones were mortised into the earth; and on a boulder a cement frog, the size of a young calf and the color of Paris green, with a mouth gaping as richly bright as a split liver on a butcher's block, crouched." (4)[3]

The more definitive characteristic of this unreality is dehumanization, apparent in the individual's attempt to live outside the human community and to maintain a demeanor of unconcern. Thus, what bothers Brad in the grotesque perversion of Happy Dell is not its unreality but the intrusion of a single real element. "Bradwell Tolliver wished that the water did not look real. What always worried you was to find something real in the middle of all the faking. It worried you, because if everything is fake then nothing matters." (4)

Like all of Warren's protagonists, Brad is in flight from the reality of involvement. In Fiddlersburg, his major attempt to flee the world is a fanciful romance with Leontine Purtle, whom

2. Arthur Mizener, in an excellent analysis of *Flood* to which I am indebted, argues that the flood is "the irresistible flow of time." "The Uncorrupted Consciousness," p. 692.

3. John E. Hardy finds the Seven Dwarfs Motel "the allegorical setting of phony traditionalism" because of a medieval element in its decor. "Robert Penn Warren's *Flood,*" p. 486. The emphasis of the scene, however, seems to be on the various ways in which things have been twisted out of nature.

he conceives as the Lady of Shalott, cut off from reality by her blindness, and thus suitable for his escape.[4] He sees her attractiveness in terms of water imagery. After her ride in the Jaguar, he asks Yasha, " 'Did you notice how she could really let go . . . and flow with you like she and you were sort of flowing downstream together, sort of nudging each other with the tide?' " (126) Later, in another idyllic dream of will-less abstraction, he thinks of being with her as "drifting, side by side, down a gentle current. . . . If you just drifted you would drift into some calm place where you would lie side by side, out of the current, and the current would go past and carry with it everything that had ever happened, like the trash and plunder sluiced away on the crest of a freshet." (361) When they begin to make love in the Candy Cottage of the Seven Dwarfs Motel, Brad seems to have made good his escape. He "lifted his left knee and drew the sheet taut like a tent and with his right arm anchored the cloth over their heads. They were inside the tent, and the world was outside." (361) In his affair with Leontine, Brad becomes one with the Seven Dwarfs Motel, relinquishing whatever remains of his own reality as he signs the register with an alias.

When Leontine's diaphragm, another mechanism of unreality, reveals that she is neither Snow White nor Lady of Shalott living at a virginal remove from the world, Brad takes his characteristic refuge in cynicism. " 'Don't you like me any more?' " Leontine asks. He answers, " 'I like you just fine, girlie.' " (367) In fact, he likes her not at all, for he sees her as part of the corrupt world of experience, and the nature of his private hell is such that he loathes that world and flees from any contact with it even as he yearns to escape from his isolation and gain such contact. His failure is inevitable, and whether he fails to escape the contact or fails to escape his isolation, he responds with angry cynicism.

Brad fails to escape contact with the world when, earlier in

---

4. Hardy makes the interesting suggestion that Leontine is "a savage caricature of sentimentalized Southern Womanhood." "Robert Penn Warren's *Flood*," p. 486.

his relationship with Leontine, she compliments him on the compassion in his short stories. Instead of feeling pleased, "he felt trapped. He even felt a constriction of breath." (231) When she proceeds to tell him how the book had opened her to the world, "he rose abruptly from the big Morris chair. He found that pudgy, enclosing softness intolerable." As he tries to escape the chair's symbolic "enclosing softness," his response is anger. " 'What's it like,' " he asks, " 'to be blind?' " (232)

Brad tries to achieve contact with the world very rarely, but he tries and fails to escape his isolation when he stops for gas at the Seven Dwarfs Motel and addresses the Negro attendant, a complete stranger, with the words, " 'Must be some high old times in Happy Dell.' " The narrator describes Brad's expectation: "The chamois would pause on the windshield and, in that moment of male connivance, of animal camaraderie, the face would grin through, servile but sly." The attendant, however, like Jerry Calhoun's bell-hop, rejects the attempt at contact; when the grin proves not forthcoming, Brad demands, " 'They have to pay you much to wear those trick pants?' " (6) Caught in his own ambivalence, Brad can only writhe in torment and hide that torment in a pose of cynicism.

The origins of Brad's torment are revealed in considerable detail through a series of mental flashbacks, for Brad's flight from the world, like Jack Burden's, Manty Starr's, and Jeremiah Beaumont's, involves a flight from the past which returns to haunt him. We learn, first, of Brad's early break with his father, Lank Tolliver, who, as Brad says, had come boiling out of the swamp into Fiddlersburg. As a boy, Brad accepts his father until he learns that Lank disappears into the swamp neither to hunt nor to whore, but to lie weeping in the mud. Lank, it would seem, cannot adapt to Fiddlersburg and its modicum of culture; as an indoor pastime, he burns the household books leaf by leaf. More specifically, Lank cannot accept the version of himself which Fiddlersburg has created. He longs for his old identity and the innocence of allegiance to objects and urges.

Brad's boyhood is shaped by the books which he fights to save from his father's brutality and by the brutality itself. He "had been held to the father by that very brutality, and had learned to play upon that brutality as on an instrument." (176) Lank's cruelty frees Brad from the burden of filial love. He makes Izzie Goldfarb his surrogate father; he is outraged to discover that Lank lapses from cruelty to tears and thus unwittingly makes a claim on his feelings. The knowledge that his father weeps in the mud "tore at some fundament of his own being. He would wake in the night, and feel, actually, sick." (176) But Brad does not respond to the claim. He uses his secret knowledge as a weapon against Lank which enables him to go first to a private school and then to college; when his father dies, he cannot weep.

As an undergraduate, Brad writes a short story entitled "I'm Telling You Now," in which he bids goodbye to Izzie as he had neglected to do on leaving Fiddlersburg. The story grows into a collection; through his feeling for Izzie, Brad discovers and communicates the humanity of Fiddlersburg's residents. The collection is published, and critics, we learn, comment on the book's compassion. Leontine Purtle, describing the book's effect on her, says, " 'It was like I knew that people were alive and something was going on inside them. And inside me, too. I had always felt sort of frozen inside, I guess. . . . That story— it made me want to reach out and touch the world.' " (232) With this book, Brad has clearly entered Warren's real world of human involvement.

Through publication of the book, however, Brad meets the editor Telford Lott, who becomes a second surrogate father to Brad and misleads him from his contact with the world toward unreality. Telford Lott is a believer in high causes, and he takes Brad from humanity to the idea of humanity. Lott makes Brad aware of having no ideology, no self-image, no story, and, as the narrator informs us, Brad decides to fight in Spain in the attempt to remedy this deficiency. The narrator further indicates the error of Brad's decision: "He did not realize that as soon as he began to try to create, to enact, a story for Bradwell Tolliver, he would lose that gift, the only one he had, of recognizing the story of someone who had no story." (68) The creation of such a story is of course quite unreal; Brad does not reveal his plan beforehand because "to tell about it would be

like trying to tell a dream." When he finally does reveal it, he
"felt very cold and austere." (137) Thus Brad breaks his tie
with humanity, and, returned from Spain, cannot understand
his own malaise. "He had believed in the justice of his cause.
So he did not know why he now woke in the night and felt that
all his experience came to nothing." (142) When he considers
going back to Spain, "he thought, with a flash of elation, of
killing a faceless enemy. Then, in that split second, the faceless
enemy wore the face of Telford Lott." (145) Lott and Spain
merge as faceless humanity, abstraction, unreality.

Through Telford Lott, Brad meets Lettice Poindexter while
he is at very low ebb as victim of Lott's causes and of New York,
Warren's unreal city, where Slim Sarett and Isaac Sumpter
have previously been relegated to fade out of being. Brad has
himself begun to fade. Discarding his previous day's prose output, he thinks, *"If I can't do better than that I better quit."*
And with that thought comes a glimpse of the void, "for, suddenly, he was thinking, too, that if he was not a writer then
he was nothing, he was not real, he did not exist. He stood
there in the cold terror of nonexistence." (134)

In his love for Lettice, Brad finds a new form of false being.
As he visits his closed-up house in Fiddlersburg to prepare it for
his arrival with Lettice, his mind shapes the story of someone
who has no story and he feels a deep calmness. "It was as
though he, Bradwell Tolliver, were discovering a buried self. It
was the true self that would live forever." (195) This "true
self" with its immortality is of course an impostor, for the
true self is wholly contingent; Brad's immortal self is the self
which Jack Harrick finds so appealing in *The Cave*. For Brad,
too, this false being proves temporarily satisfying. Marriage
seems to have removed him from the unreal world which had
threatened inundation; thus, in his first months of marriage, "the
world seemed to fall away from his life, leaving it in its balance
and perfection." (209) This removal from the world seems
quite enviable to Maggie, who says, " 'There was the picture,
too, of what Lettice and Brad were. How they seemed to exist
in some sort of perfect freedom, like birds in the air.' " (249)
But the Fiddlerburg idyl, however pleasurable, is itself unreal,

as Lettice comes to realize. She says to Brad, " 'Maybe we shouldn't ever have come to Fiddlersburg. Maybe it was just a dream I had of being with you in the dark, out of the world.' " (334) The unreality of the dream comes to claim Brad entirely. Maggie notes that, the second summer, things had changed: " 'Brad had been making a new gang of friends, young engineers on the TVA dams up in Kentucky.' " She tells Yasha, " 'Lettice and Brad didn't seem to belong in Fiddlersburg anymore. They just lived there, and people came from outside and drank and played poker. Or bridge. Even from Nashville or Memphis, sometimes with girls.' " (250)

Brad's writing loses the compassionate contact with humanity which had been its strength. He is at work on a story about an acquaintance, Jibby, a story which later becomes the movie "The Dream of Jacob." Maggie describes the movie to Yasha: " 'A man like Jibby who comes in and marries a girl like Rita Jackson and treats her badly and gets killed by an old colored man on the place who is devoted to the girl and won't say why he has killed the husband—dear God, it was an awful movie!' " (250) The accuracy of the judgment becomes clear when Maggie continues with an account of the real Jibby, who " 'wasn't killed. He just drifted to nothing. He didn't know anything about farming. He threw money around and mortgaged Rita's land, and even with high wartime prices, lost the place and they moved away. She looked like an old woman by then.' " (250) Here Maggie inadvertently indicates the failure of Brad's melodrama; he has missed the human element in the episode, and so has missed the real story, and has, in fact, written of a dream.

The spiraling descent into the void reaches its nadir with Brad's drunken porch party, where Alfred O. Tuttle, overcome by alcohol, Lettice, and the mesmerizing music of a stuck record, rapes the dazed Maggie after Brad, thoroughly besotted, has dragged Lettice off to the bedroom. The sexuality of the scene is an appropriate culmination to Brad's romance with Lettice, which had in effect begun when they spied a woman masturbating in Central Park. Their marriage, based on sexuality, is fruitless; Lettice, like Leontine, uses a diaphragm. Their sexual act is a parody of love, from the early months in New York when Brad instructs Lettice to " 'Hang that thing on, gal,' " to the cave-men tactics of the porch party. Brad and Lettice, like the characters of *The Cave*, use sexuality as their cave, their haven from reality. Their sexual encore, after they have decided on a divorce, reveals the abstract, unreal nature of that escape. Performing "in a sardonic trance," Brad finds that "It was very confused and numb and strange, but in the end like plunging into the black center of things, where nothing equaled nothing." (335)

A year later, Brad returns to Fiddlersburg and begins a novel about Cal's trial, in which he attempts to grapple with the human situation; he discovers that he cannot. The result of this approaching confrontation with reality is fear. When an offer from the Coast comes, together with Maggie's plea that he not use this material, Brad takes advantage of the opportunity and flees westward, like Jack Burden, in search of innocence. What he finds is apparently some seventeen years of unreality. A second marriage terminates in divorce, and Brad thinks, in retrospect, "It was that he simply didn't care. Had he ever cared? . . . Maybe if she hadn't cared so much they would have made it." (25)

The action of the novel begins at the end of those seventeen years, with Brad trying to maintain his cynical veneer of indifference to deaden himself to past and present unreality. As he goes to the airport to meet Yasha, who has hired him on the strength of "I'm Telling You Now," he passes the Seven Dwarfs Motel, which supplants not only dogwood and sycamore, but the spot where he and Lettice held their postmarital liaison. He thinks of Lettice in spite of himself; "bird-song filled the ears, and heart, of Bradwell Tolliver, and he tried not to feel anything." (9) He fights the memory, but when it finally wells up, he recalls dialogue in which he had also tried to feel nothing. Offering herself as encore, Lettice asks, " 'Wouldn't you like to remember us really ourselves?' " (30)

"God damn it," he cried out, with a burst of bitterness like an abscess breaking in the heart, "I don't want to remember a God-damned thing!" (31)

His false being torments Brad. Memories of his father, Lettice, and Izzie Goldfarb recur, because in each case he has failed to maintain the human contact which would make him real. His contract to work with Yasha soothes him only until he learns that he has been hired, not on the basis of his seventeen years' output, but on the strength of "I'm Telling You Now." Waking up in Fiddlersburg, he "knew the source of his despair."

Long ago he had written a little book. Now, because of that book—not because of *The Dream of Jacob,* which last night had been on a million marquees, not because of two Oscars or one award from the Screen Writers Guild, not because of seventeen credits, not because of any of these things that had filled all the years between—he was here and Yasha Jones was here, and they would make a beautiful moving picture. Had all the years between gone, therefore, for nothing? (59)

Thus the question of his own reality, of his existence, comes to focus on the movie he is making with Yasha. He thinks, *"If I don't make this picture right, I am a failure. I am a failure, and good."* For a moment, this thought surprises Brad. "He had never had it before. But he felt, suddenly, that the thought had been there a long time, solid and objective like a rock or a post, and his face had been averted from it." (77)

And yet, although Brad recognizes the significance of his script on Fiddlersburg, he does not understand that the source of his failure and long malaise lies in his abstraction from the world. Thus, even while he tries to succeed in Fiddlersburg, he continues to flee human involvement. Talking to Leontine, he goes so far as to deny any emotional directive in "I'm Telling You Now." He tells her, " 'The fact is when you are writing a story or doing a movie script, you hit some logic, not the heart business, that drives you to a certain end. It is like chess.' " (231)

"The Dream of Jacob," in its awfulness, is, then, like chess, as is the script which Brad does for Yasha. Finishing it, "he knew that there wasn't a bolt out of place or a nut loose. He let his mind run over the thing, not the content, just the wonderful clean shape of it, and felt delighted with that shapeliness." (340) Yasha, too, applauds its shapeliness, its mechanical perfection, but rejects it because it lacks compassion, or what Brad has called "the heart business." Yasha says, " 'You have done nothing more expert. . . . But . . . it is not you. It is only the *you* who is an expert. . . . What matters is the feeling. Where, in this . . . is the feeling we want? Where is Fiddlersburg?' " (341–343)

Brad's response to the rejection is to blame the world, saying that he has been " 'crassly deafened by the clamor of mere factuality.' " (392) When Leontine encourages him to try again, he says, " 'If a man gets his leg shot off, it is not much use to start again to grow a new one. He had better get a fancy prosthetic limb from the Veteran's Administration, and practice a lot and learn to do the rhumba with it, and give exhibitions. . . . He will be an expert.' " (353) Brad blames the world for deafening him and shooting his leg off; he does not yet realize that the problem is not too much contact with the world, but too little.

The events that follow the rejection of his script seem to confirm Brad's view of the world and its destructive experience. The dream of a pure life with Leontine apart from the world collapses with the discovery of the diaphragm, and it is completely expunged by Jingle Bells, who refers to her as "that blind tart." Just as the Gingerbread House, Candy Cottage, the Seven Dwarfs Motel, and Happy Dell are grotesque parodies of nature, nature twisted by some dream, so is Leontine as Lady of Shalott, and so is Mortimer Sparlin as "Yassuh Boss" darkey in the fool's garb of Happy Dell and as Brad's "Jingle Bells." When the attendant shatters the dream of Leontine, and with it, the dream of darkeyism, Brad is at least partially aware of the discrepancy between conception and actuality. He tells Leontine, after his scuffle with Jingle Bells, that there was an argument about change. Then, reflecting, he says, " 'Yeah, change! . . . Yeah, that's a great one.' " (365) In each case the change from dream to reality seems to be a change for the worse: from Lady of Shalott to blind tart and from obsequious darkeyism to vicious callousness, from subhuman to inhuman.

The ensuing encounter with Abbott Sprigg seems to offer still further confirmation of the world's destructiveness. Brad sees in Abbott's face a strange doubleness: "There was the face of a handsome boy, with dark, glowing, anguished eyes and very glossy black hair and skin pale and smooth as marble on the brow, but over it was hung, somehow, the face of a fat man with cheeks and throat sagging, the color of warm tallow." (369) Once again, the world of reality seems to have corrupted some fundamental, if unreal, beauty, and Brad goes floating off to the swamp rat Frog-Eye, who lives, as his name suggests, in watery freedom from the world's burden. After Frog-Eye drinks himself into a stupor, Brad "heard the whirr and tingle of the life of the swamp darkness that seemed to fill the world." (377)

As in Warren's other novels, the protagonist is not alone in his false being. Chief supporting victim is Yasha Jones, who, according to the narrator, "had, for some years now, lived in the joy of abstraction." (264) His appearance is symbolically appropriate. The pattern of scars on his skull forms what is described as an abstracted world, "a pale, bleached-out, pink, ghostly continent on a somewhat elongated, parchment-colored globe." Like Bogan Murdock in *At Heaven's Gate*, Yasha is an artifact; his skull is "like some piece of precious china that has been shattered, then painfully and scrupulously reassembled and glued." (20) Even photographs reveal Yasha's withdrawal from the world. Brad remembers that "the head of Yasha Jones was always, in those few photographs, slightly bowed, the gaze was veiled and the head seemed to float, with its exotic intellectuality, bodiless." (15)

The dam, Brad's Jaguar, and Yasha's camera are all one as miracles of modern technology, the unreal products of an unreal vision. The camera, then, is the symbol of Yasha's unreality. Like Brad, he hides behind technique. He sees people primarily as images on film, and mercilessly strips them naked in his mind's eye; repeatedly, in the course of the novel, he views life in terms of panning and zooming. He has achieved a form of transcendence over the world, and he brings his camera to Fiddlersburg because he sees, mirrored in the town's movement into unreality, the unreality of his own transcendence, "that difficult and austere thing that, because it was all he had salvaged, he called joy." (105) He thinks, "Now, even this late, he had stumbled upon this place, and its doom, and the place and doom would give him—in spite of, no, because of, his very abstraction from place and event—the perfect image of his pure and difficult joy." (100)

Lettice is another figure of false being. Her rejection of her mother—" 'a bitch,' she said simply"—parallels Brad's rejection of his father, who, he tells Yasha, " 'was a son of a bitch.' " Her early interest in Telford Lott's causes is one form of escape; her painting is another; still another is her psychoanalysis with Dr. Sutton, also unreal, with "aqueous bifocals" (149), and "grayly lunar face" (151), who finally decides that he himself needs analysis. Yet another escape is her devotion to sensuality. Her dressing table, as described by Maggie, is a ritual altar to unreality:

"I suppose of all the relics of that life the thing that fascinated me the most was her dressing table. My God, it was ten feet long . . . and it had a million jars and bottles and atomizers and boxes on it. There was a case with, I promise you, not less than forty lipsticks. Everything was gold and glittery. Perfumes I had never even heard about. Creams and powders and astringents especially prepared for her in Paris, with her initials on the cases.

She would spend hours, too, at that table, doing things to herself. To give Brad a treat, she would say." (214)

The minor characters are similarly caught up in the unreality of detachment. Cal confesses to Brad, " 'Maybe I was hell-bent on being a doctor just because I felt I couldn't talk to people. Not to any people, really. . . . Maybe I felt if I made them well they'd be grateful, things would be different.' " (281) Blanding Cottshill is ready to flee from the world when he plans to go to Scotland and " 'not get mixed up in things.' " (380) Maggie seems to have married Cal in the hope of emulating Brad in " 'the dream come true' " (325) ; of her cloistered life with Mother Fiddler after Cal's imprisonment, she says, " 'I know enough to know that the way I lived all those years wasn't what they call normal. Maybe it was all crazy.' " (337) Another fugitive from the world is Mortimer Sparlin, Jingle Bells, who seems to have forsworn humanity in his humiliation of Brad, but who, afterwards, presses his face into the bedsheets, apparently longing for union, and thinks "of falling into blackness, for he did not know what was left." (365) Still another fugitive is Mr. Budd in his delight with the rising water. "He looked down and thought of water rising, and a grim joy filled his heart. He thought how the water would rise all around, and only the pen would stick up out of the water, and how he would be here alone where he had always wanted to be." (170)

Mr. Budd, in his commitment to the rising water and the isolation it will bring, is doomed to unreality; salvation—real existence—comes only with a commitment to others, a sharing in the human communion, a sense that all human actions are intricately interrelated. Abbott Sprigg apparently gains such a realization. He tells Brad that in Fiddlersburg he has discovered the actor's prerequisites of humanity and compassion, and, in his subsequent success, he seems to have entered the human communion.

Blanding Cottshill also seems saved from unreality. He goes to the penitentiary to see Pretty-Boy and, in his words, " 'tell the poor murdering, tear-drenched, blood-stained, irrelevant and immaterial, illiterate banjo-picking black bastard goodbye.' " (381) Later, he rejects his plan of going to Scotland, asking Brad, " 'After Fiddlersburg, where can a man go, anyway? And feel real?' " (426) He buys a farm nearby, knowing that he will be asked to take the controversial case for school integration, that he will be "mixed up in things."

Cal is also saved and tells Brad about his blazing discovery in solitary confinement: " 'You realize in that flash that there is no *you* except in relation to all that unthinkableness that the world is. And you yourself are.' " (412) Thus Cal can accept himself and the world, and when Brad mentions that Maggie is pregnant, his response is not outrage, but pleasure. We last see him in his prison laboratory, but he clearly has not lost himself in its routines. He begins to explain his experiments to Brad, but quickly stops, saying, " 'I don't want to beat your ear off. It would be just technical stuff. I guess you wouldn't understand all that crap.' " (414) He has learned that, as against a human tie, his experiments are just "technical stuff."

Maggie, too, is saved. During her seclusion with Mother

Fiddler, her awareness develops; she says, " 'It was only later on I began to get the feeling that everybody was caught in some sort of web.' " (331) She comes to recognize " 'the crazy tied-togetherness of things' " (332), the interrelatedness of all actions, the great web of being that so confounds Jack Burden. When she says to Brad, " 'You are my dear Brother,' " (393) she seems to speak out of her new sense of the human tie.

Yasha, like Maggie, has developed his awareness even in his unreality. At one point he thinks "how, for some years, his concern with his craft had been a way, his only way, of feeling himself into the world. But now, this moment, he thought how this concern with the ways of his craft—had it become, rather, a flight from the world?" (189) Maggie and Yasha are saved through each other; their awareness has prepared them for the love which alone is fruition of awareness, and which alone makes them real.

Among the more important characters, then, Yasha, Maggie and Cal seem to be saved. Warren's "salvation," however, is precarious, for, in his own words, "the victory is never won." [5] The endless nature of the struggle for reality explains why Brad and Lettice, whose struggle is examined in greatest detail, seem, in the end, to remain seekers.

Prior to her marriage, Lettice's psychiatrist tells her, " 'You are a Puritan idealist. Unfortunately your Puritan idealism does not square with your compulsive sexual rivalry with your mother.' " (139) We never learn whether Lettice does in fact feel any rivalry with her mother, but the remainder of the diagnosis, concerning a conflict between Puritan idealism and sexuality, seems borne out in a scene which follows very shortly. As she pushes a lock of hair from her face, Lettice notices the action in the bathroom mirror, together with her "flicker of pleasure in the sight." Her response is to pick up a razor blade and prepare to cut off the hair which has offended by pleasing her. This rape of the lock is prevented only because in her

5. Robert Penn Warren, " 'The Great Mirage': Conrad and *Nostromo*," in *Selected Essays*, p. 54.

imagination she sees "the blade slash across the right cheek, not once but twice, splitting that smooth, subtly gleaming surface." (141)

Lettice's innermost attitude toward the flesh is further revealed in the dream which she recounts to Maggie in her letter. In that dream, three masked men appear in the great, lonely hotel suite she inhabits, with the apparent aim of hanging her. These three men, figments of unreality who come to make her unreality complete by destroying her, are presumably Telford Lott ("the tall skinny one with the high thin head and big bony hands"), Dr. Echegaray ("the short one that limped a little"), and Brad ("the burly middle-sized one with broad shoulders and round, thick-skulled head"), who gooses her into jumping. It would seem that to Lettice with her latent Puritanism, the dream's conclusion of falling forever has religious significance; her fall results from her carnal transgressions.

Lettice's life twenty years later as Catholic lay worker in a home for the aged seems to be another mortification of the flesh, a realization of the vision in which she slashed her cheek. She takes satisfaction in describing her gray hair cut carelessly short, varicose veined legs in elastic bandages, and slimness gone to fat (" 'one hundred and seventy pounds by golly!' "). The joy afforded her by her work seems akin to Yasha's in its austerity, as she seems to realize when she contrasts it to the unattained joy with Brad and writes, " 'I feel that it would be wicked (am I wrong?) to deny the possibility of that joy, but at the same time I am grateful to God for all that has led up to this joy I now have.' " (432) Like Miss Idell in *Band of Angels,* Lettice moves from one extreme to the other, and seems, at best, in command of a particularly precarious equilibrium which the narrator only partially approves.[6]

Unlike Miss Idell, however, Lettice is no fanatic. Her puzzling

6. John L. Longley Jr., however, argues that Lettice is fully redeemed, in that "bodily decrepitude is wisdom and grace." "When All Is Said and Done: Warren's *Flood,*" in *Robert Penn Warren: A Collection of Critical Essays,* p. 173.

over the question of joy suggests that she is still a seeker, and her life of menial work in an old people's home indicates that she has gained a very specific interest in others. Furthermore, she seems to recognize her past involvement in life and to accept, at least implicitly, her responsibility for Maggie's marriage and for the porch-party disaster. She writes, " 'And don't think I don't know now that nobody can just keep his wicked foolishness private, and I flung mine around something awful.' " (429) Lettice, then, has broken out of her unreality, but her reality seems incomplete, and of a secondary order.

Brad, whose successful struggle against detachment is the most closely detailed, begins to emerge from false being with his visit to the swamp, for even in Frog-Eye's unreal world he cannot escape reality.[7] From Frog-Eye he learns two things, both having to do with responsibility. First, he discovers the extent of his own responsibility for the porch-party disaster and its consequences years before, which he was then too drunk to remember. Second, he finds that, like Sugar-Boy in *All the King's Men,* even the degenerate Frog-Eye is capable of moral responsibility through a sense of shared humanity; Frog-Eye tells how, that night, he stole in to rape Lettice, saw her weeping, and left.

Coming out of the swamp, Brad is even more tormented. He meets Blanding Cottshill and watches him go into the penitentiary to say goodbye to Pretty-Boy. "Brad Tolliver sat there in the Jaguar and was overwhelmed by rejection and envy. He felt rejected by life. He envied the man who had a reason to go up the hill and up those stone steps and enter that dark door. He had no reason." (383) Going home, Brad meets Maggie and Yasha returning from their tryst and longs to share in Maggie's joy. Out of this longing to be a part of mankind, Brad tries to stop Cal from shooting Yasha, though the act is one that he cannot understand. When they thank him afterwards, he thinks, "You do not know what to say when someone thanks you for an act you have performed but do not know the motive or the

7. John L. Stewart notes that reality pursues Brad to the swamp, where Frog-Eye tells him about the porch-party. "The Country of the Heart," p. 255.

meaning of." (421) He also fails to understand the change in
Cal or Cal's explanation of that change, wondering only how
Cal would respond to the knowledge that Yasha has been responsible for the improvement in the penitentiary medical
facilities.

The actual birth of Brad's awareness occurs on the day of
celebration and lament over Fiddlersburg's demise. The tone
is elegiac in this communal confrontation with the void, but
Brad remains detached. He sits in the cemetery, apart from the
crowd, and seeing the wrecking crane beside the church, the
vision of disintegration which shapes much of the novel fills his
mind: "A few whacks, and it would be nothing but a pile of
broken brick. That would be tomorrow, and tomorrow Bradwell
Tolliver would be far away. And, he told himself, he would not
come back." (416) His torment remains; his hand keeps stealing
to the telegram from Mort Seebaum contracting for the Fiddlersburg script, assuring him of his place in an unreal world of
"images on a screen," as in the movie theater where he has spent
the previous afternoon. His torment increases when he sees
Leontine pushing her father in his wheelchair; as he watches,
"the crowd opened, and the chair and Leontine were swallowed
up." (419)

The acceptance of Leontine into the crowd makes Brad more
consciously alone. He remembers a dramatic moment of isolation
from his past. Sitting in a drugstore telephone booth, he had
been suddenly aware of the people passing outside. "Trapped in
that glass box, in its icy glitter, he could not breathe. He felt
that he was doomed to stay there forever, while the air got
thinner and thinner. He could call out, but nobody, not one of
those people outside the glass, nobody in the world, would
hear." (420) Then Brad begins to read Maggie's letter and
the letter from Lettice.

Before he can read very far, Blanding Cottshill comes up and
tells how Pretty Boy has been able to face the electric chair with
Mr. Budd's help and that he himself plans to stay and "get
involved in things." With these indications of human ties, Brad
resumes his reading of Lettice's letter, and, learning how altered
her appearance has become, begins to understand the unreality

of their past. The reported change affects Brad profoundly; with his image of Lettice as voluptuous sexual object slipping away, he begins to see the real woman. Further evidence of the unreality of that image comes as, in the letter, Lettice retells her dream. According to her implicit analysis, she falls through carnal sin. A more objective analysis of the dream suggests, however, that the fall, like Sue Murdock's dream fall in *At Heaven's Gate,* is simply the plunge into unreality which is a life based upon empty sexuality and thus parodying the true human communion.

The letter shows Brad that his relationship with Lettice was unreal—that beneath the sexual image which they both created and called Lettice Poindexter was a human being, sharing in his struggle for reality. Stunned, Brad "slowly began to realize . . . that now, for the first time in all the years, even in the years of the contact and the clutching . . . Lettice Poindexter was real to him. She had really existed. Somewhere, in her way, she existed now. He marveled, slowly, at that fact." (436) This thought leads to another: "He wondered if the fact that he had not known she was real meant that he himself had not been real." (437) Overcome with self-doubt, he wonders, "God, would he be a crip?" a question with distinct symbolic overtones. "No, Dr. Harris had said, no, he would be as good as ever." (437) Thinking of what he has been, Brad is overwhelmed with self-loathing. He protests to himself, *"But I have done good things!"* (437) And he wishes he had died in Spain, so that all would have known of his goodness.

He hears Brother Potts praying and the town singing his song about the blessedness of their lives, "and then he thought how Brother Potts had won his race against the rising waters. Brother Potts had done what he had set out to do." (438) With that thought, Brad suddenly recognizes the nature of his own unreality. "With that thought came the thought that everything he himself had ever done, the good and the bad, had been like the grimace and tic and pose and gesture of the crazy man, who, by repeating the empty form, tries, over and over, to re-establish the connection that had existed before the weight of ice broke the wires." (438)

Lettice's story and Brother Potts's triumph lead Brad to realize that experience can be redemptive as well as destructive. With this awareness gripping him, his will is reborn, and he thinks, "At least a man didn't have to twitch and jerk and pule and mutter and twist his fact in craziness and call it all something else. At least a man did not have to lie." (439) Brad drops his walking stick, takes out the telegram from Mort Seebaum, and tears it up. The telegram represents his successful career of unreality, beginning with "The Dream of Jacob"; it is the ice breaking the wires, the lie which Brad had earlier termed "the truth of the self." (256) Brad has learned that the self does not have to be a lie. He drops his stick to tear up the telegram because his successful elaboration of the lie has been a crutch preventing him from walking on his own legs.

Earlier, when Yasha rejects his script, Brad views himself as "an expert," a man with an artificial leg. The leg, however, is real; the true self, though buried, exists. Through awareness, the unreal self is destroyed and the rebirth of the real self begins. Brad listens to the crowd singing.

He stood there and heard them. For, over the years, he had run hither and yon, blaming Fiddlersburg because it was not the world and, therefore, was not real, and blaming the world because it was not Fiddlersburg and, therefore, was not real. For he had not trusted the secret and irrational life of man, which might be the truth of man. . . . For he, being a man, had lived, he knew, in the grinning calculus of the done and the undone.

Therefore, in his inwardness, he said: *I cannot find the connection between what I was and what I am. I have not found the human necessity.* (439)

Brad has learned that life is not a mechanical "calculus of the done and the undone," a simple balancing of books (418), as he had thought earlier with regard to finding Izzie's stone and making the payment of his last respects. The "human necessity," making life more than mechanical transaction, integrating past and present, self and other, into an organic reality, is a sense of involvement in the struggle of all men for real existence, a feeling of *caritas*. Brad has learned not only of his previous unreality, but of this human need when, with tears in his eyes, he looks over the crowd of people trying to salvage something real from the wreckage of Fiddlersburg and thinks, *"There is no country but the heart."* (440) .

Flood, then, is about the reality of the heart's country, and the unreality of the heartlessness, the detachment which permeates most of the novel. It is remarkable, given as many characters as *Flood* contains, that they should all seem so alone. Blanding Cottshill, Maggie, Yasha, Brad, Lettice, Frog-Eye, Mr. Budd, Pretty-Boy—despite the novel's flux, all seem to exist in a vacuum of perfect isolation. The lives of Warren's characters are shaped by the attraction and repulsion they feel for this vacuous, unreal existence: attraction, because it frees them from the burden of involvement and responsibility; repulsion, because its loneliness is more than they can bear. As Mr. Budd says, speaking of a man in solitary confinement, " 'He can't stand just being himself.' " (158)

The great causes of Telford Lott, the sexuality of Lettice, Leontine, and Brad, the violence of Jingle-Bells, Pretty-Boy, and Brad in his accusation of Maggie, are all attempts to gain isolation and achieve some sort of purity and freedom beyond the welter of experience. They are, at the same time, abortive attempts to break out of this isolation, for such ambivalent behavior is the paradox of human existence. The resolution of this paradox, the only cure for the disease of unreality, is awareness and involvement. Brad, like all of Warren's saved, goes home to the country of the heart; renewing "the connection that had existed before the weight of ice broke the wires," he repairs his broken link with mankind.

CHAPTER IX

Meet Me in the Green Glen

BEGINNING WITH *All the King's Men,* Warren's novels present the true love which arises only with selfhood; the description of false love begins even earlier, with *Night Rider* and Mr. Munn's interest in Lucille. The central concern of *Meet Me in the Green Glen* is love, both true and false, but particularly the romantic dream of love. This love, the idyllic conclusion to countless novels and films, the love of "and they lived happily ever after," is the green glen, the place of enthrallment.

The glen is, literally, Spottwood Valley, and its inhabitants—Cassie Killigrew Spottwood, Sunderland Spottwood, Cy Grinder, and Murray Guilfort—are spiritual as well as literal residents. Cassie's early, unconsummated romance with Cy Grinder, revealed through flashback, is chronologically the first representation of the green glen. Cy is in flight from his origins, so that for him the romance is a dream of courtly love. He treats Cassie as object of adoration, beyond reach until he can transcend the contamination of his family. He plans to rise to the level of his lady by completing a correspondence course in engineering; he cannot have her, he thinks, until he is "translated out of himself, no longer the son of Old Budge, but an untarnished Adam walking the new earth with the breath of the Worldwide Correspondence School blown into him." (77)

Cy's new self dies aborning when Mrs. Killigrew, spiritual

counterpart of Matilda Bingham in *The Cave,* discovers the romance and delivers a merciless tongue-lashing, in which the shortcomings of his family figure prominently and in which she suggests that Gladys Peegrum—whose inelegant surname attests to her flaccid unattractiveness—is the appropriate mate for such a degenerate as he. Her diatribe is galvanic; he listens in silence, for he "knew that he had lived among shadows and delusions and that the words that fell from that bony apocalyptic face were the blaze of truth. Nothing he had done, or could ever do, would change the truth." (79) In that "blaze of truth" he leaves Cassie with neither a word nor a backward glance, for he has a new vision of unreality to replace the old; "he would ferociously act out his destiny, which, as he now saw, was to need nothing." (80) He drops his study guides down the privy hole and leaves Spottwood Valley to fulfill his nihilistic destiny. After eight years of wandering, he returns only to prove that his destiny is complete and that Spottwood Valley now means nothing to him. "He could move through it, now, spit on its earth, and not see it." (80) Sitting over the privy hole which Budge had used and which houses the study guides of the Worldwide Correspondence School, he sees the way to "crown his destiny"; he marries Gladys Peegrum.

The end of the romance has a similarly destructive effect on Cassie, who lives from that time on "with the sense of having no role in the world, no identity." (81–82) Less than a year after Cy's departure, she fulfills her mother's dream by marrying Sunderland Spottwood, who, as roaring sensualist, views her only as sexual object; she, in turn, detests him. She gives herself to him initially in an unreal daze, in which she sees him as Cy Grinder. After four years of such unreality, she has a nervous breakdown—or a sudden access of awareness—when she bursts out laughing at her mother's funeral, and is institutionalized from 1942 to 1946. During this period, Cy returns to Spottwood Valley and marries Gladys Peegrum. Imagining them together, Cassie articulates the fragmentation which has claimed him, and her as well. "In her intuited understanding of the vengeful alienation of Cy Grinder from himself implicit in the act performed upon Gladys Peegrum, she found confirmation of her own rejection of that other Cassie who had been her then-self, and who had once quivered under his touch. What a little fool that then-self of Cassie had been!" (81) In 1946, Sunderland has a brain stroke which leaves him paralyzed and speechless, and Cassie is released to serve as his nurse in the decaying house.

The house is sustained by another figure of the void, Murray Guilfort. Murray is haunted by nothingness, as an early visit to the Spottwood house dramatically reveals. Looking about the house and thinking how little change has occurred, he suddenly realizes that "everything, even as he looked, was changing. The shreds of the carpet raveled under his eyes, writhed like worms in anguish, burning in their lightless combustion. The leather of the Bible disintegrated and fell, like pollen, on the white marble of the table top. The paint scaled off the eyes of old Sunderland Spottwood, the arrogance fell away from those painted eyes in miniscule pale flakes that lay on the dark brick of the hearth, like dandruff. Everything was nothing." (35)

In his flight from nothingness, Murray becomes a master of false love. As a young man he marries Bessie solely to further his career, and through his cold indifference he kills her. His relationship with Cassie involves a different form of false love. He meets her at the Spottwood house while she is still there in the capacity of nurse; "out of the shadows, shyness, and distance, the face had floated at Murray Guilfort, who, in that instant, twenty years ago, had inarticulately, but with an angry wrenching of the heart, recognized his destiny." (33) He makes this instant the substance of an enduring dream, which, as his impossible "destiny," leaves him the victim of an unkind world. Even as this dream continues, Murray enters a new phase of false love under the tutelage of Alfred Milbank, who advocates the sensual life. Describing the performance of his call girls as art, he instructs Murray that " 'illusion . . . is the only truth.' " (23)

In the attempt to gain that truth, Murray assumes the role of sensualist. Sophie is a success, and Murray, like Jack Harrick in *The Cave*, feels "strong and immortal." (25) The replacement of Sophie by Mildred troubles Murray only slightly, but the news of Milbank's sordid death in a hotel room checks his sense of immortality, and he contracts "a severe gastric disturbance."

The sexual realm receives still another shock when Murray learns that Mildred has married, and the new girl is to be Charlotte. "But at the thought of Charlotte, a nameless fear had gripped him, and the strange discomfort which the doctor had said was a symptom of pancreatitis again began." (27) Although Murray does not realize it, he is experiencing anguish as the dream proves inadequate to fill the emptiness of his life. With the sexual domain discredited, his need to dominate the void takes a new form; he decides to become a justice of the Tennessee Supreme Court.

Murray's dream of Cassie and his dream of sexual immortality have common origin in his idolization of the young Sunderland, which stems in turn from his conception of Sunderland's indomitable sensuality mastering the void. To Murray, "the flushed face, the blazing glance, the ruthless self-fulness had been . . . its own confirmation, the fulfilment of life beyond all the deceptions and niggling of the world." (133) His "image of Sunderland Spottwood was that of an angry, laughing self clamped astride a great beast that reared triumphantly against a world of nothingness." (34) Milbank in his sensuality is simply a Sunderland surrogate, as the animal imagery indicates; he is "horsy" and has a "raw, neighing laugh" (21, 23). Cassie, in turn, is Sunderland's, to Murray, and his fancied feeling for her can only be explained as an extension of his envy for Sunderland.

It is that envy which forms the basis of Murray's financial support for Sunderland and Cassie. Just as Murray sees in the image of Sunderland's vitality the measure of his own failure, so he sees in the fact of Sunderland's paralysis the measure of his own triumph. Looking at his old friend, Murray experiences a "burst of cold, justifying joy. He had felt the moment that justified all. It was Sunderland Spottwood who lay there." (44) In a later visit, as he looks into Sunderland's eyes, once "like the flame of a Bunsen burner," now "the sad sick blue of skimmed milk," he feels "a surge of dizzying elation . . . as if justice had, at last, been achieved." (134) Out of this friendship which is hatred, Murray embarks both on the love which is sexual mastery and on the love—the adoration of Cassie, spiritual nurse—which is total surrender of being, imagining himself in Sunderland's place receiving Cassie's ministrations.

Cassie, Sunderland, Cy, and Murray, then, all represent the green glen-valley and its unreality. At the symbolic heart of the valley's unreality lies Sunderland, paralyzed, like Jack Harrick in his wheelchair; both are symbolically stricken. Cassie, too, is paralyzed; Sunderland says, " 'You—you're bottled-up crazy.' " (92) The decaying Spottwood manse completes the symbolic pattern; in its "dark hollowness" (4), it is another version of the cave. The narrator makes the analogy between the house and the void explicit when he notes that "it is not possible to caulk every crack, nail up every rat-hole, seal every window casing and perfectly defend the dark inner nothingness." (51) Cassie and Sunderland live in the house, Cy lives in a poorer version of the house, and Murray assumes the protectorship of the house and feels drawn to it because all have lost themselves in the void. Angelo, looking down into Sunderland's eyes, feels that "they were looking up at him, they were alive, they were sucking him in. It was like losing your balance, falling into a deep hole." (157)

The action of the novel begins with the arrival of Angelo, who, although a stranger to Spottwood Valley and the Spottwood house, has found his spiritual home. While Cassie is sitting in the house staring at the window, so lost in the void that she cannot distinguish inside from outside, memory from fact, and her face, "very white, seemed to be floating there, bodiless" (8), Angelo—another of Warren's angels—appears, coming down the road "trying not to think of anything." (6) In flight from Sicilian revenge and, more important, from his own sense of guilt, he settles into the emptiness of the house with a certain amount of satisfaction, happy "to hide himself . . . in this unreality." (46) For "if certain thoughts or images came into his head, he would start sweating or shaking. Therefore, it was wise to cultivate the blankness of being." (51)

Although Angelo finds his new life of unreality comforting, he is also troubled by it, so that he makes abortive attempts at flight. One such escape is his pursuit of Charlene. As he watches

her move up the path, "she flamed into reality." (53) Walking
with her, he is surprised to find "that she was real. Not a dream."
(60) Another escape is the day's labor; "every morning was, in
its own way, a flight into occupation." (49) Perhaps most revealing is the escape which occurs in the early weeks of his stay,
when he literally flees the farm and the task of hog-butchering
which he and Cassie perform.

> Then, all of a sudden, the woman straightened up from the big pan
> of entrails, fixed her gaze upon him in a moment of recognition that
> became, in a flash, nonrecognition, and moved toward the house. He
> straightened up too, saw the bulk of the house floating dark and
> motionless in the chill brightness of air, saw the figure moving away
> from him, saw the darker spot where the earth had soaked the blood,
> saw the scraped baby-pink of the carcass.
> He turned and fled. (48)

Angelo's subsequent reflections on his flight indicate that he
does not merely flee blood, entrails, and carcass: "it shook him
because he became aware that he had fled from something just
discovered in himself that he did not know the name of. Something had stirred in the depth of black water, for an instant
glimmering white like the belly of a fish, as it turns. Something
had breathed in the dark." (49) The imagery itself is con-
clusive; the dark, watery, inner cavern is clearly the void, as is
"the house floating dark." Angelo flees "the chill brightness of
air" and its indifference, which is Cassie's, in her "recognition
that became, in a flash, non-recognition," in her "moving away
from him," and his own as well, in his seeing her only as "the
woman." Insofar as he runs from the carcass, it is, like the chill
air, a sign of his spiritual death.

These flights, however, all lead back to the house. Angelo's
literal flight ends with the realization that he has nowhere to
go. The relationship with Charlene, although—like all the relationships in Warren's novels—rich with the possibility of discovering another, of an 'I' encountering a 'Thou,' is stunted
by Angelo's unreality. Even the day's work leads Angelo back to
the house, for with that work he becomes its custodian. The
house increasingly claims him, and he begins to feel curious

about it. As he explores the master bedroom, imagery of water and darkness once again defines the atmosphere of unreality. "His own shadow, cast by the candle held breast-high before him, made the darkness darker behind him. There his shadow filled the air, enormous, hovering over him. . . . Out of the darkness, the furniture swayed slowly at him, swaying into the light of the candle like clumps of waterweed in the backwash of a sluggish current." (106) His major project during this phase of false being is, appropriately enough, repairing the plumbing of the house. As he lies in the crawlway beneath the house tracing the pipes, "he felt a lassitude creep over him, rising from the earth beneath him, like water rising, and then, as the deliberate flood seemed to close over him in the dark, he knew that it was peace, a nothingness that was, strangely, a kind of sweetness." (116) His ritual morning rape of Cassie is no more than an affirmation of this nothingness. He is occasionally troubled by the emptiness of their contact, at one point crying out in frustration, " 'Who you? . . . *Porca Madonna!* Who you are?' " (103) But their relationship in this first phase remains mechanical. Readying himself for the sexual attack, in his deepened alienation from self he thinks of himself as *"the man,"* and of Cassie as *"quella cretina."* (69) The orgasm itself is empty; "the spasm seemed impersonal in its automatism, not involving him, as though it were not even happening to him." (71) Later, he thinks, "It was like she was not real. No— . . . it was like you, you yourself, were not real." (113)

For Cassie, too, this phase of their relationship is unreality. When Angelo returns to the house after his flight, "In her sight he seemed to sway and swim there, as though the darkness from which he had come were a medium like water sustaining him. It was as though the pressure of all that darkness flooding down the hills and woods had just pushed the door open, and in one second more, would come pouring in, filling up the room, washing him at her." (98) When she hears the sounds of Angelo exploring upstairs, she thinks, "him." *"Him,* for he didn't have a name, at least not in her mind. Even if he had told her his name, as she knew he had, she never called him by it. He was no name, he was the shape with no name: *him."* (109)

The second phase of their relationship begins when, with Murray having jealously informed Cassie of Angelo's past, she goes for the first time to Angelo's room in the evening and says, " 'Tell me your name.' " (130) In the story of his imprisonment, she has seen her own void. She tells him, " 'I thought how all my own life, it was like that, like being locked up, and lying in the dark—' " (148) As Cassie realizes that her life has been "like being locked up" and "lying in the dark," she realizes that the void is shared. She goes on to tell Angelo, " 'It was all of a sudden then that I knew—I really knew—how you felt. It wasn't till I knew how I had been always locked up that I knew how you felt—' " (148) Cassie has gained the reality of selfhood. Awakening the next morning in Angelo's bed, she tells him, " 'I feel I just got born.' " (153) Like all of Warren's reborn, she has a new vision of the world. " 'You look different,' " she tells Angelo. " 'Maybe it's because I never saw you before.' " She then adds, ' 'Maybe I never saw anything in the world before.' " (154)

Although Angelo resists Cassie's offer of reality, it finally seems to affect him. When Cassie first enters his room to share her new vision, he feels angry, and pictures himself provoking her into sending him away; he pictures himself once again walking the road alone. "He felt a kind of angry joy in that image, a sense of being himself again, free again." (129) In her altered attitude he senses some coming change which he dreads, for it comes "just when he had found a way to live in that changelessness." (129) Cassie, trying to draw him into her new vision of context, places a hand on his forehead. What touches him, however, in his continued flight from context and the betrayal of his countryman Guido, is Cassie's repeated assertion that it was " 'not your fault—not your fault—oh, no—it wasn't—' " (140) Cassie offers him involvement, but what he hears is the promise of continued freedom from his past; in his mind he cries out, *"Senti, Guido— listen—non è colpa mia—she say not my fault—she say me innocente—innocente—"* (140) Yet the love which Cassie offers finally seems to convey its reality to Angelo as, while Cassie talks, he feels his protective walls—which Warren has built of wood this time, to accord with the house—collapsing, "as though something inside had cracked like a piece of dry, dusty wood under a great slow pressure." (149)

Even this crumbling of the walls, however, is not unambiguous, for they crumble when Cassie assures Angelo of his freedom to leave the house; although this is symbolically the freedom to join Jack Burden and emerge from the closet of history into the creation of history, to Angelo, Cassie offers only the freedom from himself. Whereas the new phase of their relationship is, for Cassie, an escape from illusion into reality, for Angelo it is a new form of dream, to be carefully nurtured. He molds Cassie into a sexual plaything, buying her a whore's outfit of scarlet and black and teaching her the technique of love-making, together with its forbidden words. In this act of creation he finds the sense of power with which to fill the void. In the narrator's words, "In the end it was her ignorance that possessed him. It was the emptiness that he had to fill up. . . . Filling it up, molding it, breathing it, eating it—that was his way of being alive. He lived by her ignorance. When he taught her something, he felt the thrill of his own knowledge, her own power." (177)

Once again, this dream world, while insulating Angelo from his past, frightens him in its abstraction from the world and from time, so that he enlarges his sphere of false being by absorbing himself in the objective reality of an alternate, daytime life involving farm tasks. "He was dimly aware of some need to grasp first one project, then another, as some new image of the future. . . . To get through the day, he had to pack it with moments that seemed to be stolen from the future, that seemed to promise a world that would have a future." (181) In his fragmentation, he rigorously separates the worlds of day and night. Thus, he conquers the impulse to tell Cassie of his plans for the farm, because "the tractor was real, the field to be plowed was real, the cows would be real, and deeply, darkly— in something like despair—he knew that you could never carry what was real, and belonged to the day, over the secret line into the world that was a dream and belonged to the night." (171)

Angelo nearly gains the awareness that would unite these two worlds when, having mastered the tractor, he comes to the house early for a drink of water and, for the first time in weeks, sees

Cassie in her baggy brown sweater and brogans. With that sight, "he realized that everything else—the red dress, the black patent-leather slippers, the black lace of the panties and brassiere on her white skin, the bottle of whiskey held to her lips, the wrenchings and contrived tensions, the forbidden words she had humbly learned to utter, the calculated frenzy—all had been a lie . . . a lie he had told to himself." (190) He begins to see anew. "He looked across at her and thought, marveling, how he had never really seen her before." (190) For the first time, he calls her by her given name. But then he catches the scent of her perfume, which reminds him of a girl in his guilt-ridden past, and this much reality proves more than he can bear; he flees to the dairy house and Charlene.

The major event of the novel, which, like Jasper's misadventure in *The Cave*, affects each of the characters in different ways, is the murder; following that, in what is perhaps a weakness of *Meet Me in the Green Glen*, Angelo and Cassie are no longer central as they move in different directions. Angelo's letter to Cassie from prison seems to indicate that he has finally gained selfhood; he awaits death fearlessly. Cassie, on the other hand, draws back into her unreality. Several years after the execution, when Cy talks to Murray about her, he says, " 'The truth has done gone and changed on her. She's got a whole new kind of truth.' " (355) To investigate, Murray goes to the sanatorium, where a robin outside "would not stop its mellow, drowsy, petulant note: *gluck*, silence, then *gluck*, like water dropping." (356) Cassie offers her hand, which seems "dry, cool, boneless. To his pressure the hand was as unresponsive as a small rubber glove filled with sawdust." (355) Her new kind of truth, Murray finds, is the belief that Angelo has not been executed, but rather, as she tells Murray, " 'has gone away. . . . Somewhere far away, and he is happy.' " (359)

Murray moves to center stage after the murder, to become the primary example of absorption into unreality. The imagery surrounding that immersion is explicit. When Cassie informs him that Charlene is Sunderland's daughter, he responds by "gaping like a fish." (216) When he returns to the Spottwood house, he takes pleasure in the thought that "soon, when the land lay under the dark suffocation of water, there would be nothing to remember." (351) As he goes through the house for the last time, "his body drifted from room to room, slowly, weightlessly, as though floating through that medium." (351) After Miss Edwina censures him and he hears that Angelo has been executed, "he stood there, and in his interior darkness a tide, black, thick as slime, and nameless, was sluggishly flooding upward. . . . All night the viscous, lightless tide would be slowly rising in him. It would be like an internal drowning." (333)

Fleeing from Cassie's happiness, Murray goes to spend the night at his wife's house, where his sense of the void pursues him and finally forces itself on his consciousness. Cassie has spoken to him of love, and, as he sits in the study, "the word rang hollowly in his head as in a great cave." (365) He goes out of the study into the hall; "the walls of the house seemed to be slowly constricting," and the high chandelier "was hanging above him like ice in a dark cave." (366) He thinks, "He was in himself and could not get out." (366) He recalls Cassie's question, " 'Did you ever love anybody, Murray Guilfort?' " and "For a moment, frozen on the stair, in the darkness, he started to cry out: 'You!' " Then a ray of recognition comes: "he knew it was a lie." He thinks how "long ago, the door of the old Spottwood house had opened and there was the white face of a girl floating toward him in the shadows . . . and that was all he had ever known: a dream. It was the dream he had been forced to dream." (367)

Awareness strikes still deeper as he goes to his bedroom and thinks of Bessie, and of how she had loved him even knowing that he had married her only for money and status. "Well, if she loved him—and he tested the edge of the thought like sliding your thumb down the honed edge of a knife—her love was the mark of her inferiority, her failure." (369) Then he begins to see the situation whole. *"And of mine,* he thought, even as he desperately tried to stop the thought: *of mine!"* (369) He manages to stop the thought with another: that Bessie's love, going unrewarded, was no more than an illusion. *"Love,* he thought, *so that is love.* To dream a fool dream like that fool

Bessie Guilfort, to dream a fool lie like that fool Cassie Spottwood, to dream a lie and call it truth." (369) His next thought,
that they have in fact experienced truth as he never has, over-
whelms him by confirming his sense of his own unreality. In a
daze, he gets into bed, downs an overdose of sleeping pills, and
falls away from reality completely; "he sank deeper, sinking
into truth, into the truth that was himself, whatever his self was,
as into joy, sinking there at last." (372) Like Ikey in *The Cave*,
he is fully at one with his false self in its void.

The development of the true self is shown primarily through
the characters of Angelo's defense attorney, Leroy Lancaster,
and Cy Grinder. Leroy, unlike the other characters whose
thoughts the reader shares (Cassie, Angelo, Murray, Cy), is not
literally a product of Spottwood Valley, but he is a victim of
unreality nonetheless. He dreams, as a young man, that Corinne
will prove sexually tempestuous; on their wedding night he is
only partially disillusioned when "she gave herself to him sweetly,
gravely, graciously." (270) Nearly twenty years later, after
Cassie's courtroom confession, he imagines himself spying on
Corinne, and suddenly feels the abstraction of his life from
reality. "He wondered where life had gone. He thought: *When
will I be done with illusion?*" (272) He goes to his office, where
his musings explain his unwillingness to go home; within the
framework of his dream, he is a failure. At first he does not see
that his dream is his failure; he wonders whether Corinne married him because he had the smell of failure and would therefore
serve as object of charity, or whether her charity had made him
a failure. As he sits there feeling "demeaned, outraged, emascu-
lated," he has a startling revelation: "blazing in the darkness of
his head," he sees Corinne in the old sexual fantasy, this time
with Angelo as her partner. "After a moment, sitting, he knew
that that afternoon, in the courtroom, his own eyes had fixed
upon Angelo Passetto as unforgivingly as those of the juryman
from the hills. He had wanted Angelo Passetto to die." (277)
He realizes that he has been one with those who "stared un-
forgiving" at Angelo "from the thorny shadow of their own
deprivations, yearnings, and envies" (275): that he shares in
the dream and its destructiveness. *"Me too,* he thought, sitting

there, shivering. *Me.*" (277) With a new vision of unity, Leroy thinks, "God forgive me—I have blasphemed against my own life." (278) By dreaming his dream he has hated himself for his inadequacy, hated Corinne as the source of his inadequacy, hated Angelo as the measure of his inadequacy. Leroy, then, is ready to go back to Corinne and a new life; "slowly he became aware that he wanted to go home. That was what he wanted to do. Somehow, he felt that he could go home now." (278)

Cy Grinder also emerges from his unreality. The process begins when he stops with Cassie in a roadhouse after their unsuccessful attempt to see the Governor. She tells him what might have been: how they might be an old married couple returning from a visit to their son at the University. His response is to lurch from the table and bolt for the restroom. Staring into the mirror, he begins to discover his place in the context of the world and time. Stricken with that glimpse of true being, unable to face himself or anybody else, he locks himself in a stall. "Cy Grinder stood and thought how his whole damned life had been working to bring him here to stand shivering, locked in a can like he was afraid, saying *now, now,* for if you could just live now, no backwards and no forwards, you could live through anything. But a man can't. He was finding out that a man can't." (324) Alone with that knowledge, Cy experiences a moment of anguish. "Something was like a big hand reaching through his ribs, a hand big enough to grab his heart like a wet washrag and squeeze it into a wad, and then that hand was tearing his heart out by the roots while he stood there in that atrocity of anguish and could not breathe." (325)

After the trial, as Game Warden of the new Reservation whose lake is to cover most of Spottwood Valley, he comes to an accommodation with reality which results in a limited contentment. As Game Warden, like Angelo, he tries to absorb himself in the world of fact. "He had learned the trick of thinking, every night before trying to sleep, of what he could do the next day, what task he could turn his hand to, where he would go on the Reservation. So he almost never thought of the past." (340) The thought of the prospective lake pleases him. "Cy began to feel that the past itself would be flooded . . . that part of his being was already under water, and he thought of the shadowy depths with a kind of cold contentment." (341)

Several years later, however, as he sits up sleeplessly, the past forces itself upon him through the television news and its report of Murray's apparently successful attempt at suicide. This intrusion of his context fills him with a loneliness which draws him to the bedside of his daughter, whom he adores, and then to the bedside of his wife, whom he does not adore. "Before he turned away to undress, he realized that the face on the pillow was very much like the face of the little girl who lay in the next room. He had never before observed that fact." (374) For the first time, Cy sees the web of being, with its physical and temporal relationships. "Then he was wondering if there would ever come a time when the little girl in the other room would be heavy and slow-footed and short of breath and would lie sleeping . . . beside a stranger who, wakeful, was listening to her breath and did not know or care who she was. The thought was to terrible to bear." (375) Momentarily, he flees to the void; "he closed his eyes and tried to think of nothing, nothing at all." (376) In spite of himself, his wife's face comes into his mind. "Yes, that was was like the face of the little girl. All those years, and how had he failed to see it?" This time, the thought leads Cy to the matrix of involvement, and he sees his wife for the first time. "With the image of the woman's face so clear in the darkness of his head, he began to wonder what she thought, what she felt; and his wondering was mysterious to him. He wondered what she had ever thought, what she had ever felt. He realized, slowly, that never, in all the years, had he wondered that before." (376)

The novel begins and ends on a distinctly Coleridgean note. The opening scene, in which Cy kills a deer with bow and arrow, presents an *Ancient Mariner* tableau. Cy's act, like the ancient mariner's, conceivably blameless, is morally defined (according to Warren's analysis of the poem) [1] by the spirit in which it is performed. Cy exults, " 'The bastard—did you see

1. Robert Penn Warren, "A Poem of Pure Imagination: An Experiment in Reading," in *Selected Essays*, p. 229.

me snag that big white-bellied bastard!' " (8) The narrator emphasizes the immorality of the act by terming the deer "the creature," and Angelo adds to the implication of sanctity by responding to the deer with a mental short-circuit in the thought, "Sandy Claws!" Cy has re-enacted his destruction of Cassie and his violation of the great web of being. Angelo, by imagining Santa Claus's sleigh "with the fat little, red-nosed, red-dressed son-of-a-bitch grinning out" (7), shares in the crime, as he does more concretely by lying about the circumstances; with his vision of unreality, he is a false witness. Cassie in her turn also shares in the crime by firing her shotgun at Cy.

The final scene of Cy's conversion takes its Coleridgean tone largely from Warren's use of light and water imagery. Warren notes, in his essay on Coleridge, how *The Ancient Mariner* ends with a reversal of light-dark imagery, with darkness suddenly become beneficent, and says, "Coleridge's reversal is, I take it, quite deliberate—an ironic reversal which, in effect, says that the rational and conventional view . . . seeks truth by the wrong light."[2] A similar reversal occurs in this last scene. Cy comes to awareness late at night, and the moonlight in the scene is repeatedly described in terms of water. The moon is "swimming high" (376), its light was "leaking into the room" (374), "seeped" into the room, and "washed" across the face of his wife (375). This flood differs profoundly from that drowning out Spottwood Valley and the town of Fiddlersburg in *Flood*. The moon is antithetical, on the one hand, to the sun of the merely objective world, and, on the other hand, to the naked light bulb of the Spottwood kitchen and Cy's television tube, both of which, as artifacts of man, illuminate only "the world he has made" (373).

The flood of moonlight, as it "spill[s]" out of the sky "to fill the vastness of the world" (376), is the source of a new vision. At first, Cy resists it and stands under an oak; "the tree was only leafing now, but he felt the need for the protection of what shadow it gave." (375) As he realizes in anguish that he has never before wondered what his wife thinks and feels, as he

2. Warren, "A Poem of Pure Imagination," p. 234.

sees that that realization is "what he had to stand there and suffer" (376), he leaves his darkness and enters the great awakening light. "When the time came, he stepped out of the shadow of the tree. He looked up. There was the moon, with the sky, and the whole world, in its light." (376) This light is the redeeming light of what Warren, again speaking of Coleridge, calls the sacramental vision,[3] according to which the world is indeed "whole." The religious nature of the conversion represented in the scene helps to define Cy's transgression in the opening scene as well as the transgressions of all those who have lived false lives, unable to step out of their shadows.

In *Meet Me in the Green Glen*, then, Warren provides his most explicit statement about true being; he also focusses on love more closely than in his other novels. True love appears unchanged, revealing itself in the symbolic touch. When Leroy, after having reached awareness, lies awake with his thoughts of the injustice threatening Angelo, he takes Corinne's hand. (295) When Angelo, having violated Cassie daily, finds her reborn and feels the walls crumble within him, he reaches out for her—and she gives him her hand. (150) When he writes to her from jail, he comments on her smile when he kissed her hand in leaving, and concludes, " 'You try save me and now I kiss your hand, I thank you.' " (365)

In addition, Warren further articulates his view of false love, which appears in two forms, the love of exploitation and the love of idealization. Cy and Murray both adore Cassie in the love of idealization, which is like Manty's submissive self-denial in *Band of Angels*, particularly as she turns Tobias into a white statue. On the other hand, Murray marries Bessie for wealth and status, while Cy marries Gladys Peegrum to "crown his destiny" of living life at the very bottom; the two marriages are clear versions of exploitation. But perhaps the clearest is sexual, as it has appeared before in *The Cave*. Thus Angelo turns Cassie to scarlet and black, Murray dallies with his call girls, and Leroy fantasizes about Corinne. These loves of exploitation

3. Warren, "A Poem of Pure Imagination," p. 214.

and idealization involve, in Sartrean terms, the lover's conceiving himself as object or subject:[4] within Warren's terminology, choosing the world of fact or the world of idea. The two forms of love are finally the same, for both are the dreams which result from individual fragmentation. The two epigraphs are germane here. Whether, in John Clare's vision of innocence, the green glen of love is viewed as attainable in a pastoral idyl, or whether, in the darker vision of Andrew Marvell, it is viewed as beyond reach, in each case it is equally abstract and unreal.

True love, like false love, is an ideal, and as such, may prove a dream. But, as Warren says of Conrad's fiction, "the last wisdom is for man to realize that though his values are illusions, the illusion is necessary, is infinitely precious, is the mark of his human achievement, and is, in the end, his only truth."[5] This is precisely Murray's discovery, when, having condemned Cassie and Bessie for living their lies, he realizes that "the dream is a lie, but the dreaming is truth." (370) Loving is redemptive, whether or not returned. As Cassie tells Murray, even if the gift of the heart is rejected, " 'It doesn't matter. . . . because it . . . belongs to them anyway. Even if they just drop it and walk away, you're happy." (358) Of primary importance is the individual's rebirth, stemming from a sense of the ravaged face in the mirror, together with a sense of relationship, of *caritas,* which is, in Manty's words, "a charity deeper than what is love because it is the dark depth of the fountain from which love leaps but as the flashing spray." The state of caring is both a condition and a mark of the reintegration which is true being; as in Buber's formulation, the 'I' becomes a true 'I' only in caring.

4. Jean-Paul Sartre, *Being and Nothingness,* trans. Hazel E. Barnes, Part Three: "Being-For-Others."

5. Warren, " 'The Great Mirage': Conrad and *Nostromo,"* in *Selected Selected Essays,* p. 45.

Conclusion

THE STORY at the heart of Warren's fiction traces the search for selfhood. Thus Manty Starr begins her narrative with the question, "Oh who am I?" Jack Harrick asks, "Who was Jack Harrick?" And Jeremiah Beaumont asks, "Oh what am I?" The quest begins in the modern wasteland so amply documented by contemporary writers and described by Warren as a dark, watery void where "nothing equals nothing," a place of "terrible division" in which world and idea, object and subject, have fragmented. The struggle is lost with the choice of either, for with that choice, one affirms disintegration. If, on the other hand, the struggle is won, the fragments of the broken world coalesce into the unity of true being.

The individual seems to enter the lists under a handicap. As the cockroach informs us in Warren's poem "Colloquy with Cockroach,"

> I know I smell. But everyone does, somewhat.
> I smell this way only because I crawl down the drain.
> I've no slightest idea how you got the smell you've got.
> No, I haven't time now—it might take you too long to explain.[1]

The cockroach narrator alludes, of course, to Original Sin, which Warren defines in his essay on Faulkner as "a contamination

---

1. Robert Penn Warren, *Selected Poems: New and Old, 1923–1966*, p. 141.

implicit in the human condition . . . the sin of use, exploitation, violation."[2] Thus Jeremiah Beaumont says, " 'The crime is I.' " But Warren does not lead us into the realm of Calvinistic determinism. Although the contamination inheres in the human condition, the individual is the agent of his own downfall. As Warren analyzes the misdeed of the Ancient Mariner, that act, like Cy Grinder's act of shooting the deer, is one of original sin. The deed is defined by the spirit engendering it. Warren states in his essay on Coleridge, "Original Sin is not hereditary sin; it is original with the sinner and is of his will."[3]

The fallen will seems to follow one of two courses. One, that of the will in dominion, involves various attempts to master the void. Coleridge describes this "reprobate will" in terms of Nimrod, hunter of animals and men.[4] Jack Harrick is such a hunter, with his battlefield heroics and his bloody bear held high for the world's admiration. The will, having chosen this course, attempts to take dominion everywhere. The forms of that dominion can vary: for Jack Harrick and Angelo Passetto it is sexual; for Willie Stark and Murray Guilfort it is political; for Adam Rosenzweig and Jeremiah Beaumont it is absolute justice. These forms of power are neither exhaustive nor exclusive; it can take nearly any form, and an individual can seek mastery through several forms, as does Murray Guilfort.

The second course which the fallen will can take might be termed the will in abdication. In this state, instead of trying to master the void, the will surrenders to it, giving itself up to the flux of things. Jack Burden, in his resemblance to "a box of spilled spaghetti," is an example here, particularly in his "Great Twitch" phase; another example is Manty Starr, who views herself as victim of history's irresistible process. In either the state of dominion or of abdication, the will exists in abstraction; the individual is alienated from himself, and his abstracted will defines his false being.

2. Robert Penn Warren, "William Faulkner," in *Robert Penn Warren: Selected Essays*, p. 69.
3. Warren, "A Poem of Pure Imagination," p. 227.
4. Warren, "A Poem of Pure Imagination," p. 228.

In true being, as Coleridge states, the "reprobate will," redeemed, "appears indifferently as wisdom or love."[5] The importance of these two elements in Warren's thought is made
explicit in his essay "Knowledge and the Image of Man"; it is
equally clear in the novels, as the preceding analyses try to
indicate. For Warren, knowledge is the means to whatever grace
man can attain, serving to reintegrate world (or nature) and
idea (or mind). The reconciling process of redemption begins
with the mind's becoming aware of itself. In that confrontation,
subject becomes object, and the Cartesian dualism of world and
idea begins to dissolve. Warren, quoting Coleridge, says, "A
subject is that which 'becomes a subject by the act of constructing itself objectively to itself.' "[6] This initial phase of self-
definition involves separating oneself from others, but it is a
separation which leads to relationship by way of responsibility.
Thus Jack Harrick acknowledges that he is not simply like
everybody else and that he therefore must be responsible for his
life of illusion. Knowledge begins with such awareness of the illusory abstraction into which one falls. This knowledge, in turn,
grows into the larger awareness that the chaos of the world
merely reflects the inner void. Cy Grinder watches the news on
television and thinks grimly that "This was the world he had
made." And several of Warren's characters admit, with Manty,
that events have conformed to their dark wishes in a horrible
process of "coming true."

The explanation for this "coming true" lies in the relationship
between fact and knowledge. As I. A. Richards says, speaking of
Coleridge, "Nothing of which we are in any way conscious is
given to the mind. Into the simplest *datum* a constructing, forming activity of the mind has entered. And the perceiving and the
forming are the same. The subject (the self) has gone into what
it perceives, and what it perceives is, in this sense, itself."[7] Or, as
Warren himself puts it in his essay on Coleridge, "It is the
primary imagination which creates our world, for nothing of

5. Warren, "A Poem of Pure Imagination," p. 228.
6. Warren, "A Poem of Pure Imagination," p. 207.
7. I. A. Richards, *Coleridge on Imagination*, pp. 56–57.

which we are aware is given to the passive mind. By it we know the world, but for Coleridge, knowing is making, for 'To know is in its very essence a verb active.' We know by creating."[8] For Warren as well, to know is to create, and in knowing our wasteland world we must assume responsibility for it. Knowledge and will are intimately related in the shaping of fact. This concept forms the nucleus of Warren's vision from the beginning; it flickers through Percy Munn's mind as he wonders whether the darkness lies without or within. He does not quite realize that the void is never merely external; it does not simply confront us, but reflects us, as the child reflects the father. This involvement and responsibility is what the mind discovers in becoming aware of itself.

The discovery involves promise as well as indictment, however, for if man's inner void has engendered the external chaos, he should be able, by reintegrating himself, to reintegrate his world. In Morse Peckham's words, "The self does not emerge through the perception of order and value in the world; rather, order and value emerge from the perception of the self."[9] As the mind becomes aware of itself, time, which had seemed a swirl of events, resolves itself into a present which one can stand outside of and examine, a past from which he can learn, and a future which, on the basis of his new knowledge, he can plan for and even influence. In terms of this resolution, Nick Papadoupalous "tried to think of a day different from what today would be." Similarly, the natural world, which has seemed a random assortment of objects and urges, resolves itself into coherence. This does not mean, however, that man becomes one with nature. Speaking of Faulkner's work, Warren says, "Despite the emphasis on the right relation to nature, and the communion with nature, the attitude toward nature . . . does not involve a sinking into nature. In Faulkner's mythology man has 'suzerainty over the earth,' he is not of the earth."[10] In Warren's mythology, too, man must realize that the natural world is in his care. Cy Grinder, finally

---

8. Warren, "A Poem of Pure Imagination," p. 207.
9. Morse Peckham, *The Triumph of Romanticism*, p. 52.
10. Warren, "William Faulkner," p. 72.

seeing a harmonious world, serves as custodian of the new park. For Warren, the world can be redeemed only through such awareness of man's relationship to his world.

The harmony of a world remade is achieved, however, not only through knowledge in the form of self-awareness, but also through knowledge in the form of love. According to Coleridge, the reintegrated will appears both as knowledge and as love, and Warren says in *Audubon*, "What is love? One name for it is knowledge."[11] Self-awareness results in love, for in seeing ourselves as others see us, we develop a new empathy. As Warren states, again in his essay in Coleridge, "imagination not only puts man in tune with other men, with society: it provides the great discipline of sympathy."[12] And in his essay on Conrad, Warren describes the predicament of man by saying, "insofar as he is to achieve redemption he must do so through an awareness of his condition that identifies him with the general human communion, not in abstraction, not in mere doctrine, but immediately."[13]

This awareness is clearly not the simple mastery of information which we normally term "knowledge." Such poor power to add, subtract, and rearrange is no more than the technical facility with which Bradwell Tolliver and Yasha Jones, Ikey Sumpter and Slim Sarett all try to master the void. It is the sexual technique of Angelo Passetto, the clear intellectual light of law and Murray Guilfort. But if the knowledge sought is not mere technical facility, neither is it the visionary power attuning man to some transcendent reality which infuses itself into mind and matter. Warren is quite explicit in his rejection of transcendentalism. In his poem "Homage to Emerson, On Night Flight to New York," he anchors Emerson securely in unreality—night, airplane, New York—and notes that "At 38,000 feet Emerson / Is dead right."[14] Transcendentalism is similarly faulted through the characteriza-

11. Warren, *Audubon, A Vision,* p. 130.

12. Warren, "A Poem of Pure Imagination," p. 225.

13. Warren, " 'The Great Mirage': Conrad and *Nostromo*," in *Selected Essays,* p. 54.

14. Warren, *Selected Poems,* p. 40.

tion of Tobias Sears, who, like the Emerson of the poem, "had forgiven God everything." Warren seems in full agreement with Heidegger that *"authentic* existence is not something which floats above falling everydayness; existentially, it is only a modified way in which such everydayness is seized upon."[15] True knowledge arises not outside and above, but inside and beneath. It is largely, if not totally, what Bradwell Tolliver calls "the secret and irrational life of man": the modern unconscious: the power of imagination termed "esemplastic" by Coleridge, which fuses the fragments of being into the beautiful and true whole.

Knowing, then, is creating; self-knowledge results in love and a new vision of the world. What is ultimately involved in a new way of seeing. The world of Warren's characters conforms to their will; when they become whole they discover the real world. Thus Celia Harrick, gaining selfhood, cries out, " 'Oh John T.— I never saw you before! . . . Maybe it's because—because I never was me before.' " Jack Burden says of his completed narrative, "It is the story of a man who lived in the world and to him the world looked one way for a long time and then it looked another and very different way." Warren's saved see the world in a new light, which they provide out of their wholeness. As Coleridge says in "Dejection," "From the soul itself must issue forth / A light, a glory, a fair luminous cloud / Enveloping the Earth." This light is no more than the moonlight surrounding Cy Grinder, as he recognizes a world remade through knowledge. And it is such knowledge which Jeremiah Beaumont yearns for when he writes in his journal, " 'If we could only know.' "

The love which is knowledge is the love termed *agape* rather than *eros.* Although Warren hardly follows the Platonic bent of Denis de Rougemont, his novels demonstrate that, in the words of Rougemont, "passion and marriage are essentially irreconcilable"[16]: that the authentic relationship manifests itself not in coitus, but in the caress. In Warren's own words, "The right

15. Martin Heidegger, *Being and Time,* trans. John Macquarrie and Edward Robinson, p. 224.

16. Denis de Rougemont, *Love in the Western World,* trans. Montgomery Belgion, p. 277.

attitude toward nature and man is love. And love is the opposite of the lust for power over nature and over other men."[17] Sexuality permeates Warren's fiction, but like the pervasive violence, it always signifies the fallen world of exploitation and violation. To make possible the reality of true being, Lettice, it would seem, must renounce her sexual self to become fat and varicose. For Nick to love, Giselle Fontaine must become Sarah Pumfret, fat and sick. In less extreme terms, for Jack Burden to love, he must reject Lois in favor of Anne Stanton, with whom he can share self-awareness, a fabric of common experience, and sympathy.

Warren's words on Coleridge's wedding guest in *The Ancient Mariner* are germane here, if we take the wedding guest's levity as a profanation similar to that of sexuality. "What the Mariner tells the wedding guest is that the human love, which the guest presumably takes to be an occasion for merriment, must be understood in the context of universal love and that only in such a context may it achieve its meaning."[18]

That context of universal love is the real world. The Cartesian dualism dissolves with the realization that reality is neither solely external nor solely internal, but rather, a contextual mode of being, in the light of which world and idea are unreal fragments abstracted from the integrity of the whole. For Warren, as for Coleridge and Heidegger, the real world is one. Each part exists only in terms of every other part: relationship is all, in the elaborate and unending interaction of the web. Warp and woof, fiber and filament of that web is the knowledge which is love. When Heidegger says that man's being is care,[19] he seems very close to Warren, the two both presenting a secularized form of Coleridge's sacramental vision.

In Warren's mythology, then, derived largely from Coleridge and with distinct affinity to Heidegger, one falls from the harmony of childhood into the chaos of the world. His redemption begins with the realization that the chaos is an exten-

---

17. Warren, "William Faulkner," p. 71.
18. Warren, "A Poem of Pure Imagination," p. 256.
19. Heidegger, *Being and Time*, pp. 225–269.

sion of himself. From that realization comes a sense of involvement and responsibility, of freedom and direction, all of which define the reintegrated will and make possible a new world, an Eden which has been earned.[20] Thus, Yasha and Maggie live on a tropical island, and Cy stands reborn in his park, which is literally a new world superseding the old. That new world is precarious, however, and easily lost, for dominion and surrender are easier than responsibility. Thus Jack Burden discovers the agony of will, and Cy Grinder stands beneath the moon in anguish, knowing that that was "what he had to stand there and suffer." Because of the contamination implicit in the human condition, because of the difficulty of maintaining the freedom of responsibility, one always tends to disown his true being and join in the falling motion of the world. "The victory is never won, the redemption must be continually re-earned." "But," as Warren goes on to state in his essay on Conrad, "nothing is to be hoped for, even in the most modest way, if men lose the vision of the time of concord."[21] All of Warren's novels demonstrate that vision, through the struggles of their various protagonists. And, in still another example of the web of being, the novels *are* that vision; for, again in Warren's words, "the artistic work shows us a parable of meaning—how idea is felt and how passion becomes idea through order."[22]

The preceding chapters have been concerned with analysis, and one end of analysis is evaluation. If the foregoing analyses have any validity, they suggest at least one reason why Robert Penn Warren's fiction will endure; it deals incisively with the dissociation of being which has become a central issue of the twentieth century. Though the concerns of the novels are constant, however, the quality of the novels is not. *All the King's Men* is one of the finest novels of the century, whereas *Wilderness* is very poor indeed. Why does a novelist fall short of his own proven excellence? To Lionel Trilling, the question of such

20. Heidegger, *Being and Time*, pp. 175–180.
21. Warren, " 'The Great Mirage,' " p. 54.
22. Warren, "Ernest Hemingway," in *Selected Essays*, p. 117.

failure will remain unanswerable until we can explain success—
which we cannot do. Trilling's concern, however, is with means
rather than ends: with the psychic source rather than the results
of success and failure. These results should be open to analysis,
as Warren (and Brooks) would agree.

The most obvious criticism of an author with a fully conceived
world view holds that the world view becomes monotonous and
obtrusive. Warren deals convincingly with the question of
monotony in his essay on Hemingway, arguing that "the history
of literature seems to show that good artists may have very few
basic ideas."[23] But the question of obtrusiveness is more troubling,
since it implies that the author has sold his birthright for a pot
of message. One would expect Warren, with his contextual
theory of being, to be very much on the alert for so simple a
manifestation of idea triumphant over world, and, in fact, he is.
Arguing that the philosophical novelist is not schematic and de-
ductive simply because he has a vision, Warren says, "he is
willing to go naked into the pit, again and again, to make the
same old struggle for his truth."[24] In that struggle, the idea is
brought to earth and subjected to the world. Brooks and Warren, in the introduction to their textbook *Understanding Fiction,*
state, "The idea is important in a story insofar as it is in-
corporated into the whole structure—insofar as the story lives out
the idea and, in the process of living, modifies the idea. The
idea as an abstraction is absolute; but the idea in a story forfeits
that privilege of absoluteness, and must accept the dangers of
qualification and modification."[25] In each novel, then, the
vision is submitted to life for testing and modification. The position seems sound; to what extent is it embodied in Warren's
fiction? It might well be argued that in the novels after *All the
King's Men* the process has been reversed: the idea is not submitted to the test of life, but life is manipulated to support the

23. Warren, "Ernest Hemingway," p. 117.
24. Warren, " 'The Great Mirage,' " p. 58.
25. Cleanth Brooks and Robert Penn Warren, eds., *Understanding Fiction,*
3d ed., p. xviii.

idea. It is in this sense that *Wilderness,* for example, seems almost a three-finger exercise.

More concretely, the problem of integrating idea and form reveals itself first, in the area of plot. When Warren does not find a suitable vehicle, he cannot incorporate his idea into the events chosen. The theme then fails to make those events sufficiently coherent, and as a result they seem strung together, unassimilated, contrived, and even melodramatic. This is precisely the case in *Flood,* particularly with regard to Cal Fisher's two prison breaks; it is similarly true in *Band of Angels,* and it is applicable to a much larger portion of the plot. In discussing the problem of fusing idea and form, Warren posits the criterion of intensity, by which he means the heat produced in the fusion. We feel little intensity in *Wilderness,* in stretches of *Band of Angels,* in parts of *Meet Me in the Green Glen.*

The problem of integration also reveals itself in characterization, and here the criterion of intensity fails. We feel considerable intensity in the characterization of Jeremiah Beaumont, and yet he finally seems dull. The problem lies in the weight of philosophical introspection and metamorphosis which Warren places on each of the protagonists undergoing conversion. Some of them, like Jeremiah, simply buckle under the burden—and this explains why Warren's minor characters are frequently more successful than his protagonists, so that Skrogg and Wilkie prove more compelling than Jeremiah. It also explains why the novels which—like *World Enough and Time*—focus on a single character tend to be less successful than the novels which split their focus—and their burden of transformation—several ways. Jack Burden, who may seem to be the exception, is not. Although the focus of the novel is largely on him, it is also on his point of focus, which is the mystery of Willie Stark. Jack is saved from tedium by that mystery, as well as by his wit. And this raises yet another aspect of the problem of characterization: why are there no more Jack Burdens in Warren's fiction? Why has Warren not returned to a type of character so obviously congenial?

Warren explains his apparent preference for uncongenial protagonists, and for uncongenial plots as well, in his essay on

Hemingway. Having defined the criterion of intensity, he estab-
lishes as a second criterion that of "area,"[26] which he explains
elsewhere by saying that "other things being equal, the greatness
of a poet depends upon the extent of the area of experience
which he can master poetically."[27] In Warren's view, then, as
the philosophical novelist goes naked into the pit—repeatedly
subjecting his idea to life—his greatness depends in part on his
daring to confront new areas of experience with each descent.
All the novels after *All the King's Men* are clearly such forays
into the pit: elaborations of elements apparent—at least in
retrospect—in that earlier work. If Warren occasionally fails to
master a chosen area, we must attend to the fact, but we might
also bear in mind Jack Burden's discovery that a man's crime may
be but the defect of his virtue.

26. Warren, "Ernest Hemingway," p. 117.
27. Warren, "Pure and Impure Poetry," in *Selected Essays*, pp. 26–27.

Bibliography

The Novels of Robert Penn Warren
All page references are to the following editions:

Night Rider. Boston: Houghton Mifflin Company, 1939.
At Heaven's Gate. New York: Harcourt, Brace and Company, 1943.
All the King's Men. New York: Harcourt, Brace and Company, 1946.
World Enough and Time: A Romantic Novel. New York: Random House, 1950.
Band of Angels. New York: Random House, 1955.
The Cave. New York: Random House, 1959.
Wilderness: A Tale of the Civil War. New York: Random House, 1961.
Flood: A Romance of Our Time. New York: Random House, 1964.
Meet Me in the Green Glen. New York: Random House, 1971.

Works Cited

Barnes, Hazel E. *The Literature of Possibility.* Lincoln: University of Nebraska Press, 1959.
Barrett, William. *Irrational Man: A Study in Existential Philosophy.* 1958; reprinted Garden City, New York: Doubleday & Company, Anchor Books, 1962.
Beckett, Samuel. *Endgame.* New York: Grove Press, 1958.
Berner, Robert. "The Required Past: *World Enough and Time.*" *Modern Fiction Studies,* 6 (Spring 1960) : 55–64.

Bohner, Charles H. *Robert Penn Warren*. New York: Twayne Publishers, 1964.

Brooks, Cleanth. *The Hidden God*. New Haven, Connecticut: Yale University Press, 1963.

Brooks, Cleanth, and Robert Penn Warren. *Understanding Fiction*. 3d ed. New York: Appleton-Century-Crofts, 1960.

Buber, Martin. *I and Thou*. Translated by Ronald Gregor Smith, 2d ed., New York: Charles Scribner's Sons, 1958.

Casper, Leonard. *Robert Penn Warren: The Dark and Bloody Ground*. Seattle: University of Washington Press, 1960.

Clements, A. L. "Theme and Reality in *At Heaven's Gate* and *All the King's Men*." *Criticism*, 5 (1963): 27–44.

Coleridge's Works. Edited by W. G. T. Shedd. New York: Harper & Brothers, 1853.

Cottrell, Beekman W. "Cass Mastern and the Awful Responsibility of Time." In *All the King's Men: A Symposium*. Carnegie Series in English, No. 3. Pittsburgh: Carnegie Institute of Technology, 1957.

Davison, Richard A. "Robert Penn Warren's 'Dialectical Configuration' and *The Cave*." *College Language Association Journal*, 10 (1967): 349–357.

Fiedler, Leslie. "On Two Frontiers." *Partisan Review*, 17 (September–October 1950): 739–743.

Frank, Joseph. "Romanticism and Reality in Robert Penn Warren." *Hudson Review*, 4 (Summer 1951): 248–258.

Girault, Norton R. "The Narrator's Mind as Symbol: An Analysis of *All the King's Men*." *Accent*, 7 (Summer 1947): 220–234.

Hardy, John Edward. "Robert Penn Warren's *Flood*." *Virginia Quarterly Review*: 40 (Summer 1964), 485–489.

Hardy, John Edward. "Robert Penn Warren: The Dialectic of Self." In *Man in the Modern Novel*. Seattle: University of Washington Press, 1964.

Heidegger, Martin. *Being and Time*. Translated by John Macquarrie and Edward Robinson. New York: Harper & Row, 1964.

Justus, James H. "The Use of Gesture in Warren's *The Cave*." *Modern Language Quarterly*, 26 (1965): 448–461.

Justus, James H. Warren's *World Enough and Time* and Beauchamp's Confession." *American Literature*, 33 (1962): 500–511.

Kelvin, Norman. "The Failure of Robert Penn Warren." *College English*, 18 (April 1957): 355–364.

Kerr, Elizabeth M. "Polarity of Themes in *All the King's Men*." *Modern Fiction Studies*, 6 (Spring 1960): 25–46.

King, Magda. *Heidegger's Philosophy: A Guide to His Basic Thought.* New York: Macmillan Company, 1964.

Laughlin, James. "Introduction to 'Statement of Ashby Wyndham.'" In *Spearhead.* New York: New Directions, 1947.

Longley, John L., Jr., editor. *Robert Penn Warren: A Collection of Critical Essays.* New York: New York University Press, 1965.

Macquarrie, John. *Martin Heidegger.* Richmond, Virginia: John Knox Press, 1968.

Maritain, Jacques. *The Dream of Descartes.* Translated by Mabelle L. Andison. New York: Philosophical Library, 1944.

Mizener, Arthur. "The Uncorrupted Consciousness." *Sewanee Review,* 72 (1964) : 690–698.

Peckham, Morse. *The Triumph of Romanticism.* Columbia: University of South Carolina Press, 1970.

Richards, I. A. *Coleridge on Imagination.* London: Kegan Paul, Trench, Trübner and Company, 1934.

Rougemont, Denis de. *Love in the Western World.* Translated by Montgomery Belgion. New York: Harcourt, Brace and Company, 1940.

Ruoff, James. "Humpty Dumpty and *All the King's Men:* A Note on Robert Penn Warren's Teleology." *Twentieth Century Literature,* 3 (October 1957) : 128–134.

Sartre, Jean-Paul. *Being and Nothingness.* Translated by Hazel E. Barnes. New York: Philosophical Library, 1956.

Stewart, John L. "The Country of the Heart." *Yale Review,* 54 (Winter 1965) : 252–258.

Warren, Robert Penn. "*All the King's Men:* The Matrix of Experience." *Yale Review,* 53 (1964) : 161–167.

———. *Audubon, A Vision.* New York: Random House, 1969.

———. "Introduction to *All the King's Men.*" New York: Modern Library, 1953.

———. *Robert Penn Warren: Selected Essays.* New York: Random House, 1958.

———. *Selected Poems: New and Old, 1923–1966.* New York: Random House, 1966.

———. *Thirty-Six Poems.* New York: The Alcestis Press, 1935.

Index

$9.95 SD

WEB OF BEING

The Novels of Robert Penn Warren

Barnett Guttenberg's careful analysis of the novels of Robert Penn Warren shows that a philosophy both consistent and characteristically modern shapes their art.

For Guttenberg, "The story at the heart of Warren's fiction traces the search for self-hood." The novelist views the world's chaos as a result of the alienation of the self from itself. His fiction demonstrates ways in which individuals fail to achieve the totally integrated self. They will fail if they try to dominate the world and others — sexually, politically, or even in the name of absolute justice. They will fail also if they choose to abdicate, to surrender the will to the flux of things.

Warren's vision of redemption is one of self-knowledge, including the character's realization that the world's chaos is an extension of himself. "From that realization," Guttenberg says, "comes a sense of involvement and responsibility, of freedom and direction, all of which define the reintegrated will and make possible a new world, an Eden which has been earned." Thus, to know is to create and to make love possible.

Guttenberg points to the similarities between Warren's metaphysical position and those of Coleridge and Heidegger, for whom "the real world is one; relationship is all, in the elaborate and unending interaction of the web."

Among his conclusions is that Warren's fiction, though it may vary in achievement, will endure because it deals incisively with the dissociation of being that has been the concern of philosophers, psychologists, and other writers of our time.

The book is organized to appeal to readers with an interest limited to particular novels as well as those with a broad philosophical and critical interest.